T0169162

The Road to Power – F

This special little book will engage you, empower you, enlighten you, and enlarge you. What a wonderful gift!
Neale Donald Walsch, author of *Conversations with God*

The Road to Power – Fast Food for the Soul should live in the glove compartment and be brought out while in a traffic jam. It's concise, it's powerful, and it packs a wallop. This is a book that resolves many a paradox, and supplies the keys to the kingdom succinctly, simply, firmly with a no-nonsense attitude that is intolerant of excuses. Whiners beware, this book is not for you! For those who are really serious about living the good life on all levels, step right up and get this book. Get it for your friends. Get an extra copy for the whiner in your life. It's one of the best soul-food books I've seen.
NAPRA Review, USA

Captivating... pick up this book and start in any chapter, as each one has powerful and upbeat wisdom to help turn anyone's life around.
Magical Blend, USA

The Road to Power – Fast Food for the Soul was like a magnetic field, I was just drawn to this book. Right then and there is where the connection started. Barbara refers to this as "good energy". What I'm saying is I was meant to pick up this book like I was meant to start a connection with this incredible woman who has become a significant guide and mentor in my life. After reading her book (practically in one go), I reached out to her and that's where our relationship started. I highly recommend her books, sessions and ongoing guidance to everyone.
Karo Tak, Portugal

Thank you for the books you wrote. Just finishing *The Road to Power*. One of the best self-help books I have read.
Peter Gillespie, USA

Your book *The Road to Power – Fast Food for the Soul* is one of the most significant books I have ever read. It has meant a lot to me. I have recommended it to many people over the years, bought it many times, and given it away as a gift. I read it first time in December 2004, after hitting the wall, and it turned my life totally around from weak to strong.
Barbro Hegland, Norway

Read *The Road to Power – Fast Food for the Soul*. It brought me back on track, reading it again. Thanks for this great book...
Saad Farooqui, Saudi Arabia

Your book *The Road to Power – Fast Food for the Soul* is amazing. Thank you very much for it.
Simona Bartuskaite, Lithuania

Powerful and practical guidance for anyone undertaking the challenging journey of spiritual growth, written with a simple clarity and humility.
Eric Klein, author of *The Crystal Stair* and *Jewels on the Path*

Berger's book is my spiritual almanac. I sense what the day will bring, open her book and find some good advice and another way of looking at problems.
Jane Aamund, bestselling Danish author

Heard about *The Road to Power* some years ago and bought it. Finally read it while on vacation – and F*ck! It's just fantastic! I am so inspired by it and have already read it 4 times.
Janne Staal, Denmark

I loved your book and it saved my life... so thank you. Thank you from the bottom of my heart.
Meital Kapp, Israel

Other books by Barbara Berger

*Find and Follow Your Inner Compass – Instant Guidance
in an Age of Information Overload*

Sane Self Talk – Cultivating the Voice of Sanity Within

*The Awakening Human Being – A Guide to the
Power of Mind (with Tim Ray)*

Are You Happy Now? 10 Ways to Live a Happy Life

*The Spiritual Pathway – A Guide to the Joys
of Awakening and Soul Evolution*

Mental Technology – Software for Your Hardware

*Gateway to Grace – Barbara Berger's Guide to
User-Friendly Meditation*

The Mental Laws – Understanding the Way the Mind Works

The Adventures of Pebble Beach (a novel)

The Road to Power
Fast Food for the Soul

Book 1 & 2

The Road to Power
Fast Food for the Soul

Book 1 & 2

Barbara Berger

BOOKS

Winchester, UK
Washington, USA

The Road to Power – Fast Food for the Soul – Book 1 & 2
Copyright © 1995 & 1996 Barbara Weitzen Berger
Originally published in Denmark in 1995 and 1996 by BeamTeam Books

This edition published by O-Books, 2018
O-Books is an imprint of John Hunt Publishing Ltd., 3 East St., Alresford,
Hampshire SO24 9EE, UK
office1@jhpbooks.net
www.johnhuntpublishing.com

For distributor details and how to order please visit the 'Ordering' section on our website.

ISBN: 978 1 78535 814 2
978 1 78535 815 9 (ebook)
Library of Congress Control Number: 2017948446

All rights reserved. Except for brief quotations in critical articles or reviews, no part of this
book may be reproduced in any manner without prior written permission from the publishers.

The rights of Barbara Weitzen Berger as author have been asserted in accordance with the
Copyright, Designs and Patents Act 1988.

A CIP catalogue record for this book is available from the British Library.

Cover photo of the author: Søren Solkær

Front cover design: Tim Ray
Design: Cecilia Perriard

Printed and bound by CPI Group (UK) Ltd, Croydon, CR0 4YY, UK

We operate a distinctive and ethical publishing philosophy in
all areas of our business, from our global network of authors to
production and worldwide distribution.

Contents

To Tim Ray, with heartfelt thanks for helping make this book possible.

Book 1

1

The Road to Power

We are what we think.
We become what we believe.
Our life is what we visualize.
Our life is what we say it is.

We can change our lives
by changing our thoughts.

This is a book about power.
This is a book about the ways in which you can control your life
and create the life you've always wanted to live.

Our thoughts and words are all-powerful.
Through our thoughts and words,
we create our lives.
We are the only ones who have complete control
over our thoughts and words
because we are the only thinkers in our minds.
This is why we are so powerful.

The Revolution in Consciousness

This is the great revolution in consciousness that is taking place right now. More and more people are claiming their own power. More and more people are awakening to the simple fact that what they think, declare, and focus on is what they attract into their lives.

We are only victims of our own thinking.

If your life is not working, it's time to look at your attitudes and thoughts because only here will you find the key to taking control of your life and changing your destiny.

Decide on the life you want, visualize it, affirm it, decree it, focus on it, believe it, have faith in it, and you will find yourself living this life much sooner and much faster than you ever dreamed possible.

The Way the Mind Works

When you realize what it's all about, it's almost too simple to be true. It's almost a joke.

When the realization dawns on you, and you stop laughing, you'll probably ask yourself why you spent so much of your life working so hard, struggling like mad against outside circumstances, when all you had to do was change your own thinking.

The outside world is just a manifestation of what we choose to think about. Focus on sickness, poverty, and misery, and you will experience these things instantly. Change your focus and concentrate on the feast of life, on your blessings, on all the Good in life, on vibrant health and the abundance of the universe—and instantly they will appear for you.

What changed? The universe surely didn't. All that changed was your thinking.

The Power of Inner Work

Look around you. Most people are struggling desperately every day to survive or to perform, achieve, and succeed.

So many of us also find ourselves rushing around madly, because we believe that the harder we try, the more worthy we will become as human beings.

I know, I've been there myself. I was brought up that way, just like you were. I had the same education and heard all the same arguments we created to justify struggle. For example: That's the way the world is. You have to work hard to make it. Money doesn't grow on trees. Life is a struggle. If I work hard enough, maybe they'll love me. Old age means sickness and misery, etc.

Believing this, we desperately try to force our Good on the outer plane. Until sooner or later, we realize that it just doesn't work like that. We cannot force our Good on the outer plane. *The real point of power is inside.*

So do the inner work. Examine your thoughts and attitudes, dump the ones that don't work, and adopt the focus that will create the life you want to live.

And leave the outer plane alone.

The outer plane will take care of itself. It's like a magical computer printout of your life, anytime you press the print command, it will give you an exact reading of what you are thinking on the inner plane.

So forget struggle. Forget hardship. Forget poverty, sickness, and unhappiness. Do the inner work and start enjoying your life right now.

Practical Techniques

Since this is a book about power, each chapter contains practical techniques you can use in your daily life to gain control of your life and create the life you want to live. All the techniques described in this book have helped me improve the quality of my life at one time or another. I felt moved to write this book because these techniques helped me so much, I want to share them with you.

I tried to design this book so it's easy to use. I wrote this for busy people and for people who have little patience with long-winded intellectual discussions and/or long, boring explanations. If you want fast results, if you want techniques that are easy to understand, easy to learn and that work quickly, this book should be fun for you.

For several reasons:

First of all, this is a short book.

And second, you don't have to read the book from start to

finish to make it work for you. You can just dive into any chapter that attracts you and start there. Just follow your intuition... then this book will be happy with you too!

I've also found that different techniques have worked for me at different times of my life and that the methods I use also keep changing according to the situation, the problem, or the needs of the moment. Again, I try to follow my intuition and use whatever technique feels right.

We are all constantly evolving, growing, and changing, so we outgrow techniques or we get tired of them and release them for a while so we can move on to new methods. Likewise, a technique that worked well for us in the past can suddenly start to appeal to us again, even though we haven't used it for months or years. Then we go back and reconsider it and find new meaning, new depth, and new power. Our understanding of different techniques and ideas will constantly evolve for us, like peeling off the layers of an onion, as we continue to grow and gain power over our lives.

And finally, everything in this book is meant to give you great pleasure and a deep sense of joy. I believe that when we connect to our Higher Selves and understand that we are responsible for our lives and destinies, we see life as the great adventure it truly is and can consciously claim our own power to become the true creators we in fact already are.

2

The Power of the Force

Whatever we human beings choose to call it, our universe, our existence, our actions, our evolution are guided by a higher principle, intelligence, or power.

This power or force has a lot of different names, such as:
God
Life
The Force
The Life Force
The God Force
The Creator
Brahman
Allah
Tao
Jehovah
Our Heavenly Father
The First Cause
The Life Principle
I AM That I AM
The Presence
The Supreme Being
The Divine Presence
The Animating Principle
The Cosmic Mind
The Living Spirit
The Higher Self
… just to name a few.

Recognize the Force and Stop Resisting

When you recognize the Force and stop resisting the nature of human evolution, you will find that your entire life changes. When you realize that you are 100 percent responsible for everything that happens in your life, that your Higher Self in fact designed your life for your own soul growth, and that every difficulty you meet on your pathway through life is part of your learning process, you will experience a feeling of relief, elation, and true liberation.

You will understand that all struggle on the outer plane solves nothing. You will see that we are not victims of anything. There are no accidents in Life and no victims.

Life is a game we cannot lose because we are all here to evolve, no matter what happens.

In fact, life on Planet Earth is like going to school. This is our classroom, which we designed ourselves for our own benefit. And struggle is only a sign that we are resisting, that we are not yet doing the inner work we must do sooner or later to move on to the next stage of our evolution.

But, of course, there is no rush. You can resist as long as you want to… because there is an infinity of time… and sooner or later, you will get it.

The Universe Is Your Source

Everything in your life, my life, and everyone else's life comes from the infinite universe. The infinite universe or the God Force is the source and provides us with everything. And since there is an infinite, endless supply of matter and energy, how can we lack?

Poverty is really the failure to recognize the infinite universe as the source of everything. Other people are not your source, nor is your job, the welfare society, the government, your family, or outside circumstances. None of these things are the source of your life, wealth or prosperity. Other people and situations are the channels through which the abundance of the universe manifests in your life… but they are not the source.

Open Your Heart and Mind to the True Source

So recognize the true source of all life and abundance and open your heart and mind to greater Good, greater prosperity, increased health, abundance, peace, and joy in your life. It is always available. It is always there, just waiting for your recognition. So stop limiting your Good, your health, or your wealth by limiting your ideas or stating that you can only receive from fixed channels. For example, don't say that you live on a fixed income (in other words on your salary) because by doing so, you are closing the doors to the source of infinite supply. Realize, affirm, and visualize your Good coming to you through an unlimited number of channels from the infinite universe.

Affirm daily: I am now open and receptive to my Highest Good. The unlimited supply of the universe now pours forth to me from an unlimited number of channels. I give thanks for the infinite blessings and outpouring of abundance that are now manifesting in my life.

What is true abundance?
True abundance is all the Good
the universe holds for us:
Love
Peace
Radiant Health
Financial Prosperity
Time
Beauty
Spiritual Growth
Friends
Family
Music and Art

Joy
Nature
Wisdom and Understanding
and an infinity of more...

Why settle for less?

3

The Power of Affirmation

Do you know your word is law? That what you say, even casually, becomes your reality? I am quite sure people would be much more careful of what they say if they were aware of the power of the spoken word. You see, every word you speak or write is an affirmation. To affirm is literally to make firm. To affirm is to manifest your thoughts into material form.

Unfortunately, far too many people, not realizing the power of their words, are affirming lack, poverty, illness, and unhappiness for themselves. By complaining and proclaiming misery, they are decreeing and creating the very misery, lack, pain, and sorrow they so dislike.

Take Control of Your Words

You are the only person in your mind. You can decide, right now, to take control of your words, both written and spoken, and thereby take control of your destiny. After all, you and no one else is responsible for what comes out of your mouth. No one else can force you to speak words of negativity. It's your decision. So if you want to change your life, take responsibility for your own words right now.

Once you become aware of the power of words, you can quickly see why other people's lives are as they are. Just listen to what they are saying, to their conversations. It's very revealing. People who complain all the time, who focus on misery, who are always moaning and groaning about how difficult their lives are, do really have difficult lives. *Their lives are as they decree them to be.*

Those who proclaim joy, success, and love, those who speak positive words, who decree that good things are happening, live joyful, successful, interesting, loving lives.

"In the Beginning Was the Word..."

The Bible and other ancient scriptures all speak of the power of the word. They teach that our words are the creative force of the universe, alive with power for good or for evil.

Many modern psychological techniques also recognize the power of our words. For example, neuro-linguistic programming, an effective new technique for reprogramming our mental states, helps people change their behavioral patterns. An important tool in NLP for understanding behavioral programs is listening to what people say.

Mantras, or the use of sacred words, also aim to reprogram our minds and bodies to increased health and happiness through repeating words of power.

The world-famous mantra below was created by the French physician Emile Coué (1857–1926) to help people heal themselves of all kinds of illnesses and psychological problems. Coué, who was a medical doctor in Nancy, France, successfully treated thousands of patients with this mantra. All one has to do is repeat it aloud, fifteen times in a row, three times a day, each and every day. Repetition helps the mantra work on our subconscious mind, which then acts accordingly, without interference from our logical intellect.

Every day in every way
I am getting better and better.
Emile Coué

Proclaim Your Affirmations Aloud Every Day

You can develop positive affirmations for every area of your life. You can also use affirmations created by other people, like the Coué affirmation above. Or you can use passages from sacred texts, the Bible, or better yet, you can create your own affirmations.

Start with those areas in your life that are most pressing and begin affirming the positive outcome you want to experience. Decree life as you want it to be and believe it should be. Always affirm in the present tense. It doesn't matter if your affirmations are not yet true (have not yet manifested in the outer world). By affirming positive outcomes, you create them, first in your subconscious mind and in the universal mind, then in the outer world. Your words and your belief in your decrees make them manifest on the physical plane.

Repeat Your Affirmations 15 Times in a Row

I suggest saying your affirmations every morning and evening aloud for about five minutes at a time. If you have time during the middle of the day, say your affirmations again.

Many teachers and healers also suggest repeating each of your important affirmations fifteen times in a row, to energize yourself and give your affirmation the necessary power.

Repeating the Lord's Prayer out loud fifteen times in a row is a very powerful general affirmation.

Writing Affirmations

When you find yourself in situations where you can't say your affirmations aloud (for example, at your office, on the train), write them down in your notebook. Writing affirmations fifteen times in a row is also a powerful way to manifest Good in your life.

Be Specific

Not only should you change your affirmations to meet your evolving needs, you should not hesitate to be specific in your affirmations. It's fine to use general affirmations on a daily basis, but for specific needs and situations, be bold and affirm the results you want.

For example, to increase your income and meet your financial obligations, be definite about prosperity. (See Chapter 10 on The Power of Money.) Affirm:

I am a rich child of the infinite universe. Abundant supply now manifests in my life and I now meet my financial obligations easily and effortlessly. _____ (state amount) now comes quickly to me...

For health problems, you can create your own specific affirmations to meet specific needs or use general affirmations such as the examples below for health and healing:

My body is strong and healthy. Every day, new life, strength, and vitality are flowing to every atom, cell, and organ of my body. Every day in every way I am getting better and better and better.

I love my body and give thanks for its perfect functioning. Every cell and atom of my body now radiates vibrant health and vitality.

I give thanks for ever-increasing health, strength, and vitality. I am enjoying radiant good health now.

Affirm and Demonstrate!

As you continue to affirm, you will see the results of your inner work begin to manifest in the world around you. You will experience surprising demonstrations, unexpected changes, new Good, and an increased sense of control over your destiny.

As you begin to experience the power of your words, you can expand this power for Good by affirming Good for other people too. Often your affirmations of Good for another person can turn the tide in their life. Especially when their need seems great, do not be afraid to speak bold words of affirmation to them directly.

Say things like:
> *You will be fine.*
> *Everything is okay.*
> *You are just fine the way you are.*
> *Of course you can do it.*
> *I know you can do it.*
> *I have complete faith in you.*
> *I predict complete success for you in this venture.*
> *I admire your talents and ability.*
> *You are strong and healthy.*
> *You look so much better today.*
> *Thank you for the inspiration you've given me.*
> *I really appreciate your help.*

Such words can make all the difference to the people around you, whether they be troublesome acquaintances, good friends, co-workers, family members, children, or lovers. (See Chapter 17 on The Power of Praise and Blessing.)

Affirm and Enjoy!

Continue to play with your affirmations!

Sing them, chant them, dance to them, write them down, hang them on your walls, paste them on your refrigerator and telephones, hang them in your bathroom, repeat them silently to yourself throughout the day. I promise you that soon you will realize the full power of your words to create the Good that you so rightfully desire and deserve!

4

The Power of Release

One of the best ways to feel better is to release.

We're all carrying around such incredibly heavy loads of excess baggage, stuff we don't need, stuff that's weighing us down and preventing our Good from manifesting.

When you release, you become lighter. Releasing is a good way to raise your energy.

There are different ways of releasing:

Mental/emotional release
Physical release

Mental/Emotional Releasing

When we harbor negative emotions toward people, places, things, situations, or events, we are actually linking ourselves to them with an almost unbreakable bond. You can be on the other side of the world, but if you hate someone, you are linked to that person as if you were sitting in the same room, battling each other.

Who do such negative emotions hurt?

You!

You are the person who suffers because you're the one who's carrying around the negative emotions. You're the one who's being eaten up inside. Not only do negative emotions make you feel bad, they can actually make you physically ill and manifest in the end as ulcers, heart disease, high blood pressure, and cancer, just to name a few of the more obvious ones.

So not only is releasing a great way to make yourself feel better, you can even heal yourself of serious illness by releasing the negative emotions you have toward people, places, things, situations, events, and so on.

What Is Releasing?

Releasing is not a question of forgiving, although truly forgiving is probably even better than releasing, though harder to do. By releasing I mean just that: *You let go.* Releasing is not an intellectual exercise. You don't have to forgive the person or event, nor do you have to explain to yourself why or how or if the act of release is justified. You just do it.

By releasing or letting go, you avoid arguing with yourself, so it's an especially good way to free yourself from those people you are having a hard time forgiving.

In other words, releasing is something you are doing for your own good, for your own health and well-being, not for anyone else. You don't practice release because you are trying to be noble. When you release, you do it simply because you know that if you can let things go, if you can release negative emotions, you are going to feel a whole lot better. So all you have to do is make the decision to release and do it on a regular basis.

Remember to Release First

It's interesting to note that often people who are working with positive affirmations (see Chapter 3 on The Power of Affirmation) don't get the results they're seeking until they start releasing. This is because when we hold on to negative emotions, they do more than just bring us down, make us sick, and clutter up our minds; negative emotions fill up so much space in our lives that they can block our Good from coming to us. And when we work with positive affirmations, we are striving to manifest new Good in our lives.

You can practice releasing by proclaiming aloud or by writing any of the affirmations of release listed below.

Good Statements of Release

Some of my favorite statements for releasing troublesome people from your life:

I completely release you _____.
I release you and let you go to your Highest Good.

I completely and absolutely release you _____.
I bless you with love and release you.

I completely and wholeheartedly release you _____,
to your Highest Good.

Sometimes we feel intuitively that troublesome people are also holding on to us, so we can also affirm for them:

_____, *you completely and absolutely release me. You relax and let me go.*

_____, *you completely and wholeheartedly let me go. All things are in harmony between us, now and forever.*

If a situation or event is bothering you, you can say:

I completely and wholeheartedly release _____ *(situation, condition, relationship, experience, or event). I relax and release it.*

I now let go of any conditions or relationships in my life which are no longer for my Highest Good. I now completely let them go and they now completely let me go—for the Highest Good of all.

Releasing People You Love

Releasing the people we love is often the most important type of releasing we can do. Love of children or love of a partner that becomes possessive or that makes us try to dominate and control the other person in the name of love is always damaging. True love means liberation and frees the people we love to grow and evolve in whatever way is best for them.

For example, we might need to release a beloved son or daughter to his or her Highest Good in whatever way is best for the child, and not for us. This type of release not only brings peace and harmony in every case, it will strengthen our relationship with anyone who is near and dear to us.

In cases where you need to release someone dear to you, you might want to say:

_____ *I completely and wholeheartedly let you go to your Highest Good. I love you but I let you go. You are completely free and I am completely free. Perfect harmony is the one and only reality between us.*

Releasing Problems or Situations

Sometimes we need to release a problem or situation that has been bothering us for a long time. We might be spending a great deal of emotional and mental energy thinking and worrying about something, when what we really need to do is release it. By letting go of the problem or situation, we free it to work itself out in whatever way is best. All our thinking and worrying actually prevent the situation from resolving itself.

In cases like this you can say:

I now completely and wholeheartedly release _____ (name the problem or situation). I allow it to work itself out for the Highest Good of all concerned.

Physical Releasing

To make space for new Good in your life, it's also important to release things on the physical plane. We all have a tendency to collect things even if we no longer need them or use them.

If you have a physical, mental or emotional problem, I highly recommend releasing as much as you possibly can, also on the material plane. Let go of clothes, papers, books, furniture, and other items that you no longer use or that no longer please you. You can release them either by giving them to other people who can use them or by just throwing them away. Do whatever seems right, but let as much go as possible.

As you release old possessions, you will find yourself stirring up old energy and old emotions. It can be quite a dramatic and interesting experience. For many people, releasing possessions can be a real eye-opener. As you release, you can thank these items for serving you so well and then send them on to serve someone else. After all, everything in the universe is energy and energy doesn't like to be trapped or to stagnate. Energy likes to circulate. And you will feel better when you help it circulate.

All sickness is
basically congestion.

All healing is
basically circulation.

Releasing Attracts New Good

Not only will cleaning up your clutter make you feel better, creating new space or emptiness in your life is a good way of attracting new Good, new things, new energy, and new people into your life. It makes sense, doesn't it? Because if your life is too filled up, how will there be room enough for new Good?

Releasing, both mentally and physically, also stimulates creativity. When you let go of old stuff, old ideas and things, new ideas come pouring in. Somehow just creating the mental space for new ideas attracts them. So don't worry if after releasing people, thoughts, and things from your life, you feel completely blank or empty for a while. It's this very emptiness that is a sure sign that new Good is on its way to you. Emptiness always comes right before you get your best new ideas. Emptiness is the vacuum that attracts new Good.

Releasing Relationships

It can be the same with relationships. We can love and respect people and still outgrow them. This is not the same as rejection— we are just evolving, and people don't always evolve in the same way or in the same direction at the same time. In fact, we should thank and bless the people who have shared time, energy, experiences, and space with us on the planet, but this doesn't mean that we cannot and should not move on. When we release people with love so that everyone involved can continue to evolve in whatever way is best for them, we also make space for new relationships and new people in our lives.

When in Doubt, Release

So when you are in doubt about something, when you feel troubled, when you face problems you cannot seem to solve or resolve, or when you have an illness which lingers on, practice releasing each and every day. The results are sure to amaze you.

General Statements of Release:

I let go of all fear.
I let go of all anxiety.
I let go of all pain.
I let go of all doubt.
I let go of all sorrow.
I let go of all tension.
I let go of all sadness.
I let go of my resistance to change.
I let go of all anger.
I let go of all guilt.
I let go of all criticism.
I let go of all unforgiveness.
I let go of all hurt.
I let go of all blame.
I let go of all resentment.

I let go of my negative patterns.

I let go of my negative thoughts.

I let go of all struggle.

I let go of old patterns.

I let go of all limitations.

I let go of my negative beliefs.

I let go of the pattern in my consciousness that created this negative condition.

I let go of _____ *(name the thing, for example, this apartment, this job, this relationship, etc.).*

I bless _____ *(name the thing or situation) with love and let it go.*

I let go of the past.

I let go of the future.

I let go of my fears about _____ *.*

Choose those statements that suit your needs best and say them aloud fifteen times in a row many times a day. Or repeat them to yourself silently fifteen times or write them down in your notebook fifteen times in a row. Speaking words of release aloud is the most powerful, but silent or written affirmations are also effective, especially when you're at work or in a situation (for example, right before your next meeting) where it's difficult to walk around saying aloud, "I release all fear and doubt. I release all tension" fifteen times in a row!

5

The Power of NO

Since what we focus on increases, when we focus on the negative, we give it our power. And thus it grows.

By denying the negative, by refusing to give it our attention, we remove our power from it—and it will wither for lack of attention.

If you affirm, as Catherine Ponder suggests,

Only the Good is real
All else fades away.

you will soon realize that you do not want to give your power or attention to any type of negative input.

Say No to Complaining

When you listen to people's conversations, you find that most people are complaining about something most of the time. If it's not money problems or the weather, it's their health, their children, or their relationships. And by speaking constantly of lack and difficulties, they create more lack and difficulty for themselves.

Refuse to speak of lack or difficulties. Refuse to support negative emotions and fears in yourself or others. Pull back. Don't participate. If you can't express your feelings out loud, at least say silently to yourself: *No. No. No. I do not accept this as true.*

People will get tired of complaining—at least to you—if you don't support their complaints or participate in the conversation.

If you're brave, you can say you don't believe it's true. You might gently point out something that is good and try to shift the focus of the conversation to something positive. Why not ask instead:

Tell me every good thing that happened to you today!

Even more important: Don't complain yourself. Don't give your power to negative emotions and negative words. Every word you speak is an affirmation. Your word is law. Your words are your affirmations for your life. So what you decree and proclaim (say aloud) for yourself quite literally becomes your reality. So beware!

Don't dwell on your difficulties, problems, or aches and pains. Refuse to speak about them. Refuse to give them any notice. Refuse to give them your power. Instead, when people ask you how you're doing, tell them something good. You can always find something good to focus on and report. And when you do, this Good will grow, especially if you speak of it, proclaim it, and praise it.

If you can't find something good to say, then at least you can keep quiet. Silence is another way of saying no to the negative. By not speaking of problems and difficulties, you give them no power.

Say No to Gossip

Refuse to gossip, criticize, or speak negatively about other people.

If you praise people, even difficult or irritating people, amazing things often happen. This is especially true when you praise people who really bother you. It is as if your positive words reach them on the subconscious level, giving power to the Good in them. Again, what we focus on grows.

It works like this: When we expect people to be troublesome, they usually are. If we instead focus on their good sides, our encounters with them usually turn out to be surprisingly pleasant.

Say No to Violent, Negative Input from the Media

If we allow ourselves to be bombarded with negative input from the media—violent movies, depressing television programs, neurotic stories and articles, sad tales of woe and horror—how can we expect the Good to grow? Your time is precious and what you focus your attention on is also precious, because whatever you focus on grows. So don't give your power to violence and/or negative thought forms.

Say No to Talk of Lack

As mentioned in Chapter 10 on The Power of Money, people attract lack into their lives by complaining and focusing on their lack of money, their debts, their insufficient salaries, the high level of taxes, the high cost of living, etc. Say no to such talk of lack. Refuse to give your power to such thoughts. Instead, when people talk of lack, say (at least silently to yourself if you can't say it aloud) that you don't believe them.

Say either aloud or to yourself: "We live in an abundant, infinite universe. There is an infinite, unlimited supply of everything in this universe, including money. There is an everlasting abundance of resources in this world and money enough for everyone."

Say No to Illness

The same goes for illness. Refuse to give it any power. If you focus on every little ache and pain, every little ache and pain will grow. It's like the story Deepak Chopra tells in his book *Creating Health*.

A woman goes to the hospital with pains in her side, thinking it's a gallbladder attack. The doctors, including Chopra, open her up and discover cancer, which has spread everywhere. They close her up because they can do nothing for her. When Chopra tells her daughter after the operation, the daughter says, "Doctor, promise me you won't tell my mother. She'll die right away if she knows she has cancer." He agrees not to tell her.

The woman is discharged from the hospital and Chopra never expects to see her again. To Chopra's great surprise, she returns thirteen months later for a checkup. A thorough examination reveals no trace of cancer. When he tells her she's in perfect health, she says, "Doctor, after you removed my gallbladder, I decided I'd never be sick again."

So what is sickness anyway?

And why do some people get sick and die, while others recover and prosper?

Belief creates biology.
Norman Cousins

Our Mental States Control Our Bodies

Our bodies and our immune systems are strongly influenced by our mental states. Scientists have proven that depressed thoughts weaken our immune system. Happy thoughts strengthen us.

Norman Cousins describes in his famous book, *Anatomy of an Illness: As Perceived by the Patient*, what happened to him. He had an incurable disease. The doctors told him he was going to die very soon. He was so depressed that he checked into a hotel in Chicago and rented all the funny videos he could think of—all his favorites, like Groucho Marx. Then he lay in bed and watched the movies and laughed his head off for three weeks. Without his noticing it, his incurable disease disappeared, to the great surprise of his doctors, himself, and everyone else.

The revolution we call mind-body medicine was based on this simple discovery: Wherever thought goes, a chemical goes with it.
Deepak Chopra

In *Ageless Body, Timeless Mind*, Chopra continues: "We must conclude that the body is capable of producing *any* biochemical response once the mind has been given the appropriate suggestions... if we could effectively trigger the intention... the body would carry it out automatically."

Say No to Negative Thinking

Most people find it even more difficult to refuse to think negatively. But this too is extremely important, especially in the face of difficulties. Saying no to negative thinking is imperative.

The Ten-Day Mental Diet

Here's one good technique I found in Anthony Robbins' book, *Awaken the Giant Within*. For ten days, it is forbidden to dwell upon any negative, unresourceful, or fearful thought for more than one minute. When you catch yourself thinking about something negative or fearful, you must force yourself to focus on something that is positive or happy.

If you dwell on the negative for more than one minute, you have to start the Ten-Day Mental Diet over again.

This Mental Diet is great fun. I suggest you try it right away. It's a real eye-opener.

6

The Power of Visualization

Our power to think, conceive, imagine, and create mental images is working all the time. Whether we are aware of it or not, we are constantly picturing or seeing things in our mind's eye. We are "visualizing."

The implications of this phenomenon are enormous.

Have you noticed that people who are depressed, who think negatively, who see (imagine or visualize) gloom, doom, despair, and failure everywhere they look, usually lead gloomy, desperate lives? And that bright, cheerful people who think positively and picture (imagine) positive outcomes to events are usually successful and happy?

Whatever the mind of man
can conceive and believe
it can achieve.
Napoleon Hill

The Good News

The good news is this: We can learn to harness our power to see, picture, and imagine to create the lives we want to live.

We are all using this picturing power all the time, but most people are picturing or imagining quite unconsciously. In other words, they are not aware of what they are doing. They are not aware that they are continually imagining and picturing for themselves, for other people, and for the world in general. And if they are aware, chances are they are not aware of how powerful an effect this process of "mental picturing" has on their lives. This is very unfortunate because so many people use this power to imagine or visualize to see pain, suffering, and failure for

31

themselves when, with a little training, they could unleash the power of their imaginations to create greater Good.

Picturing Affects Your Health

Not only that, our power to picture or imagine also affects our health. This is because, as scientists have now proved, every thought we think creates or triggers a biochemical reaction in our bodies. This is why so many teachers in the human potential movement, such as José Silva, O. Carl Simonton, Louise L. Hay, Bernie Siegel, Wayne W. Dyer, Stuart Wilde, Deepak Chopra and others, teach that if we can learn to trigger or program ourselves and our subconscious minds with positive intentions, our bodies will automatically carry out these intentions. Unfortunately, most people do the opposite. But it is important to remember: "Intention is the active partner of attention. Our past intentions create obsolete programming that seems to have control over us. In truth, the power of intention can be reawakened at any time… and you can consciously program your mind… using the power of your intention." Deepak Chopra from his book, *Ageless Body, Timeless Mind.*

Blueprints for Life

Our thoughts and pictures are the blueprints we place in our subconscious minds, and our lives are a fulfillment of these thoughts, concepts, and pictures, whether they are positive or negative. Our lives on the outer plane are, in fact, nothing more than the physical manifestation of what is going on in our minds.

Persistent thoughts about sickness create sickness.
Persistent thoughts about health create health.

It's Just Your Imagination

Haven't you heard people say, "It's all in your mind," or "It's just your imagination"? Well, there's more truth to this than most people realize. And if it *is* just our imaginations, if our imaginations are such a powerful force that we can create health and happiness for ourselves by training our imagination to picture our good, then surely we've discovered one of the most powerful tools ever for improving life on Planet Earth!

So why not decide, right now, that whenever you catch yourself "picturing" a negative outcome for yourself or others, you consciously change your mental image and picture something good happening. Once you start watching your thoughts—your inner mental chatter—you might be surprised by what you discover.

Someone once said that 99 percent of what we think today is a repetition of what we thought yesterday. And if you are picturing negative outcomes… that sounds pretty serious, doesn't it?

Besides beginning to become aware of your inner dialogue and consciously trying to change it to the positive, you can do specific exercises to train and develop your ability to picture successful outcomes and to reprogram yourself, your body, and your behavior.

Visualization Exercise

Here is an example of a simple, basic visualization exercise that you can practice on a daily basis. There are many such exercises; this one just outlines the general procedure. The most important thing is to find a method you feel comfortable with and to start doing it on a regular basis.

Remember: Practice makes perfect. Your thoughts are a pool of water that has turned muddy because of all your negative thoughts and pictures. By adding clear, fresh water (new, positive thoughts and pictures), your pool will slowly get clearer and clearer. It takes a while, but sooner or later you will start to notice changes in your thinking, in your behavior, and then finally in your life.

For best results, especially if you're just starting, do the same visualization exercise every day for thirty days in a row. This is about the amount of time it takes for the subconscious mind to accept new pictures. After thirty days, you can change your focus to another subject or area of your life.

Step One: Relax

There are many ways to relax. (See Chapter 7 on The Power of Alpha.) Whatever method you prefer, the goal is to release mental and muscular tension, relax in mind and body, let go and slow down your brain waves so you enter the alpha state and open your subconscious mind to new, positive pictures and ideas. When you are relaxed, go to step two.

Step Two: Visualize

What do you want to work on? What area of your life is most pressing right now? Is it better health, success at work, a better relationship? Whatever it is, once you feel relaxed, you should create a mental picture of the positive outcome you desire.

Picture, for example, the situation or state of health you desire, in as many details as possible. *Very important: Always do your picturing in the present tense because the subconscious mind knows no past or future.* So your positive outcome should always be happening *right now*! If you visualize the outcome in the future, your outcome will always remain in the future! So see, visualize, imagine the situation you desire now, in as many details as possible. Feel the pleasure, feel the emotions your new Good will produce within you. Good health makes you feel good, doesn't it? A better relationship with your boss makes you feel relaxed and satisfied, doesn't it? Let yourself *feel* the emotions. Allow yourself to enjoy yourself and your new Good!

When you have pictured your new Good for a few minutes, let the muscles in your eyelids lighten up. Then open your eyes slowly and become aware of the room around you. You can reinforce the exercise by affirming aloud: "I am now fully awake and happier and healthier than ever before." Then resume your regular activities.

For best results, try to do the exercise every day.

The Wheel of Fortune Technique

Catherine Ponder introduced me to the "wheel of fortune" technique, another effective technique for visualizing and achieving greater Good in life. A wheel of fortune, as she calls it, is a large piece of poster board or cardboard on which you paste bright, colorful pictures of the Good you wish to manifest in your life. There are several ways of making a wheel of fortune.

The General Board: You can make one general, overall board or wheel that covers all the different areas of your life. You do this by dividing up the poster board or cardboard into four or five different areas, for example: 1) health, 2) prosperity, 3) family, 4) friends, 5) the spiritual quest. Look through books and magazines and find bright, happy pictures that illustrate the state of health, business success, family unity, etc. you wish to manifest in your life. Paste the different pictures in the area they belong to. In the middle of your board, write a positive affirmation or blessing dedicating your board to the highest Good for yourself and all humanity.

The Specific Board: You can also make specific boards or wheels of fortune for the different areas of your life. For example, you can make an entire board about prosperity, or about love, or about health. Again follow the same principle as described above. Find bright, happy pictures that illustrate the positive outcome you are going to manifest.

Important Points

Keep it secret: When you make a wheel of fortune, don't show it to other people and don't talk about it. Keep your board hidden in a secret place. You don't need to convince others that what you believe is good and right for you. It's none of their business and you don't want their criticism or negative comments to neutralize your power.

Look at it every day: Look at your wheel every single day for a few minutes when you are alone. Keep quiet about what you're doing. Do it every day.

Be careful: The power of visualization is immense, so choose your pictures with care. Don't forget you are picturing what you want to demonstrate in your life. Do not use pictures that are limiting, dark, or negative. Choose bright, bold, happy, colorful pictures for yourself. And don't clutter up your board with too many images either because it can be confusing.

Don't compromise: This is not an intellectual exercise, so you don't have to be logical about the Good you picture. Picture what you really want, not what other people want for you, or what you think you should, could or can have. Listen to the wisdom of your heart and picture what you really deeply and sincerely want to manifest in your life.

Colors: Use background paper of different colors for different subjects:

Green or gold for prosperity
White or yellow for spiritual growth and understanding
Orange or bright yellow for health and energy
Blue for intellectual achievement
Rose or pink for love and harmony

Bless your board: Dedicate your board to the Highest Good by placing a spiritual symbol or blessing on your board.

The wheel of fortune technique will help you visualize and mentally accept the new Good you want to bring forth in your life. As your new Good manifests and your life changes, you will naturally want to make new wheels of fortune to suit your new circumstances.

The Pocket Wheel of Fortune

If making a large wheel of fortune is difficult for you, or if you'd like to have something you can carry around with you during the day, you can make a secret little notebook for yourself. Follow the same technique as with the larger board. Paste bright, bold pictures in your book and write affirmations and blessings all around your pictures. Then when you have a free moment during the day, you can study your pictures to keep your mind positive and focused on visualizing your new Good.

Picture Good for Others

Not only can we visualize Good for ourselves, we can use our power to visualize Good for others, too. Just take a moment and think about how you see, picture, visualize life for the troublesome people in your life.

If you have a sick relative, do you see him getting more and more ill, do you see his darkened bedroom or antiseptic hospital room? Do you see more difficulty, more pain, and more suffering on his pathway? Or do you image him rapidly regaining his health? Every time you think of him, do you see him recovering, easily and effortlessly? Do you stubbornly refuse to pay his present illness any notice whatsoever? Do you picture him bright and cheerful, strong and healthy? Do you see the smile returning to his face and a song emanating from his lips?

Even if this is not the present situation, even if this is not true right now, you can call forth powerful, positive images of health and happiness for other people, just as you would do for yourself. So when you think of others, both near and far, why not use your power to visualize for their increased Good, too? Our thoughts are always working on the vibrational level, influencing the people around us. This is why your positive images for others act as a kind of praise and blessing on the invisible level. (See Chapter 17 on The Power of Praise and Blessing.) Don't underestimate your power to bring forth the Good in every situation for other people, too!

Mental Acceptance

As you continue to practice visualization, using the techniques described earlier, you will notice that you slowly but surely begin to *believe and accept* the pictures you have created for yourself and for others. You will notice that your belief and acceptance begin to feel natural and right, both emotionally and mentally. Then it's time to hold your hat, because when you reach this stage, amazing things start happening...

Your pictures become your reality!

Congratulations!

You just won the lottery called the Game of Life!

7

The Power of Alpha

Alpha is a great place to go
—it's better than Hawaii!

What is alpha?

Alpha is what we call the state we're in when our brain waves slow down to about half their normal frequency. This happens naturally just before we fall asleep and as we wake up in the morning. Researchers have found that good things happen to our bodies when our brains are at alpha level. Blood pressure becomes normal, pulse rate stabilizes, stressed, tense organs relax, and the body generally becomes revitalized.

This is the way scientists classify our brain waves: When we are active and wide awake, our brain waves pulsate at about 14–21 pulsations per second. This state is called beta. When we relax or are about to fall asleep, our brain waves slow down to 7–14 pulsations per second, to the state called alpha. As we enter sleep, pulsations slow down even more. Light sleep is called theta and is between 4–7 pulsations per second, and deep sleep or delta is anything fewer than 4 pulsations per second.

Beta:
14–21 pulsations per second
wide awake
fully conscious

Alpha:
7–14 pulsations per second
deeply relaxed
state of inner consciousness

Theta:

4–7 pulsations per second

light sleep

state of inner consciousness

Delta:

fewer than 4 pulsations per second

deep sleep

unconscious

The Place to Go

So Alpha is definitely a place to go. Why? Because Alpha is a natural, comfortable, peaceful, blissful, relaxed state. Everyone feels good when they're in alpha.

There are many different techniques for entering the alpha state, such as meditation, chanting, prayer, listening to soothing music, autogenic training, biofeedback, and so forth. Lots of people have their own special routines or ways of sending themselves into alpha. In fact, many people are enjoying the alpha state when they're daydreaming... they just don't know they're in alpha. There are also many relaxation tapes that guide you easily and effortlessly into alpha.

Reprogram Yourself in Alpha

One of the interesting things about the alpha state is besides being a good place to release tension and stabilize body functions, you can reprogram yourself in alpha. This means that you can change your unconscious mental programs more easily because your subconscious mind is open and receptive when you are in alpha. Many people use the alpha state to cure themselves of health problems or initiate big and small changes in their behavior and in their lives. All this is possible in the receptive alpha state.

Creative Visualizations Work Better in Alpha

When you relax and enter the alpha state and visualize the new Good you want in your life, your visualizations manifest more quickly. (See Chapter 6 on The Power of Visualization.)

Alpha opens your subconscious mind which then accepts your visualizations without any interference from your intellect. This means that when you're in alpha, you don't have to explain to yourself *how* your new Good is going to come about. You don't have to be logical or try to understand how it will happen. All you have to do is visualize your Good, and then feel and believe your Good is manifesting, right here and now.

The Silva Mind Control Method

The Silva Mind Control Method is a simple, active way of learning to enter alpha and use the alpha state to achieve your goals, heal your body, relax your mind, and solve all sorts of problems.

Here is a basic technique for entering alpha from *You the Healer* by José Silva:

1. Sit comfortably in a chair and close your eyes.
2. Take a deep breath, and as you exhale, relax your body.
3. Count slowly backward from 100 to 1.
4. Daydream about some peaceful place you know.
5. Say to yourself mentally, *I will always maintain a perfectly healthy body and mind.*
6. Tell yourself mentally that when you open your eyes at the count of 5, you will feel wide awake and better than before. When you reach the count of 3, repeat this. When you open your eyes affirm it again. Say, *I am wide awake and feeling better than before.*

There are many variations from Silva and others of this basic exercise for relaxing and entering alpha, and almost all of them work if practiced regularly.

If you are using the Silva method, once you start to get good at relaxing, you don't need to continue to count backward from 100 to 1. After 10 days, you can shorten it to 50 to 1, after another 10 days count only from 25 to 1, and finally, when you become good at relaxing, it will be enough to count backward from 10 to 1.

Once you're in alpha, you can visualize healing all sorts of problems, from minor colds to more serious illness. You can also visualize the positive outcome of all types of situations, whether in the world of business or with people who trouble you.

Guided Meditation

Here is another easy way to relax and get into the alpha state:

Sit comfortably in a chair with your feet flat on the floor and your hands resting on your thighs—or lie on your back in bed with arms and legs outstretched, palms open and facing upward.

Now take a deep breath, hold it for a while and then exhale… and as you do, feel yourself releasing all the tensions of the day.

Continue to breathe deeply and as you do, allow your attention to drift slowly to your forehead and scalp, neck and shoulders. Feel the tension flowing out of your forehead and scalp, feel your forehead and scalp relaxing. Now let the muscles around your eyes relax and as you do, continue to breathe deeply. Relax your lips and the muscles around your mouth. Let all the muscles in your face relax. Then feel your neck muscles relaxing, feel your whole neck relaxing.

Then move your attention down to your shoulders. Feel your shoulders relaxing. Just let the tension go and relax.

There is nothing to do, nothing to change, just let go and allow.

Now let the relaxation spread from your shoulders down to your back muscles, and feel the relaxation moving from your upper back to your lower back. Let yourself go deeper and deeper into a pleasant state of relaxation.

Let your chest muscles relax, and feel your heart beating calmly and easily. Relax your stomach and your abdominal muscles as you continue to breathe deeply and easily. Feel your pelvic muscles relax and feel the warm sensation of relaxation move down through your thighs, then into your knees, then down through your calves and finally into your feet and toes. Feel the warmth and relaxation all the way down in your toes.

Continue to breathe slowly and deeply and enjoy this state of total relaxation.

After a few minutes you can choose to count from 1 to 5 and wake yourself up, or you can now do a visualization exercise. (See Chapter 6 on The Power of Visualization.)

Always end by counting from 1 to 5. When you reach the count of 5 you will be wide awake and feeling much more relaxed and positive than before.

Create the Life You Want in Alpha

Once you learn how to reach alpha, you can start to use alpha to create the results you want in your everyday life. It usually takes about thirty days to master the skill. Ten minutes of practice a day is enough to begin with.

For example, say you are going to an important business meeting or job interview. Before the event, take a few minutes to go into alpha and visualize the meeting or interview in as much detail as possible. Visualize the meeting going just the way you'd like it to proceed. See yourself relaxed and happy. See yourself presenting your points in a clear, friendly manner. Visualize the other people being open and receptive to you, and reacting in a positive manner to your presentation.

Visualize a positive outcome. Then count to 5, open your eyes, and affirm that you are wide awake and feeling fine. When you've finished the exercise, go about your normal daily activities. I guarantee you will be amazed at how often your meetings or interviews turn out exactly the way you visualized them in alpha.

Talk about a powerful tool!

Avoid Negative Influences When in Alpha

It makes sense that we instinctively feel we want to avoid negative situations or being with negative people when we are in a very relaxed state of mind. This is probably because we realize instinctively, even if we don't know exactly why, that we are much more open and receptive to every kind of influence when we are relaxed.

You could say there are different levels of people... those who bring you down and lower your energy, those who are on the same level as you are and who you feel good with, and those who are on a higher level than you and who inspire you. When you are very relaxed, it's best to hang out with people who are your own level or higher.

The Healing Power of Nature

Most people also instinctively love to be out in Nature when they want to slow down and relax. (See Chapter 14 on The Power of Nature.) That's because being in Nature can also send us naturally and effortlessly into the alpha state. In addition, the restful, healing green colors we see as we walk through the woods enhance our deep feeling of relaxation.

8

The Power of Focus

Do you know what you want?

And how to get it?

Many people don't.

Not only do they not know what they want, if they knew, they wouldn't know how to get it either.

To know what you want—and get it too—is a matter of focus. In fact, the entire universe, as far as you and I are concerned, is a matter of focus.

What is focus?

Webster's Encyclopedic Unabridged Dictionary defines focus as: "the focal point... the clear and sharply defined condition of an image, the central point as of attraction, attention or activity... the ability to concentrate as *to focus one's thoughts...*"

Why do most people seem to have so much trouble focusing? Why is it so hard to concentrate one's thoughts on a chosen goal?

To be honest, I don't rightly know why because everyone can focus.

Everyone Can Focus

In fact, focusing on a goal is the easiest thing in the world to do. Focusing just means to pay attention to, and to concentrate on, something. Actually, we're all experts at focusing because that's just what we're doing whenever we dwell on a subject.

Take hypochondriacs. Even though they don't usually produce what we would call "great results" in their lives, they in fact are experts at focusing. Unfortunately for them, they are using their innate powers of concentration to focus on everything that's wrong with them, instead of turning the X-ray beam of their minds to the single-minded pursuit of some higher goal. If hypochondriacs could only become so one-pointed when thinking about (dwelling on) getting well...

To focus or become one-pointed in the positive sense of the word is a matter of choice. And wouldn't you rather be the one who's in control of your destiny, instead of letting your random thoughts control you? Because that's what happens when we use our power to focus in a negative fashion. Once you become aware of how your mind works, you can turn things around and train yourself to use your power of concentration to create and achieve what you want in your life.

So decide for yourself.

And realize that focusing is just a matter of conscious choice.

To focus means: You are going to bite your teeth into a situation, set your mind on a course, gird your loins for the journey no matter how long and arduous, and not let go until the universe delivers what you want.

If you grab it with your teeth and bite down hard, if you make up your mind that this piece of pie in the sky is *absolutely and positively* yours—right here, right now, right this minute—if you let it be known far and wide within your consciousness, if you demonstrate in thought and deed, that you're not going to let go until it happens... *it simply has to happen*. Because that's the way the universe works.

Realization on the inner plane =
demonstration on the outer plane.

So I ask you now to let the full implication of this simple mechanism sink in. Allow yourself to understand it fully and to feel the joy of attainment that this truth implies. Because if you understand this mechanism correctly, you will realize that everything you want (whatever it is) is already yours.

And it's easy as pie.

The other thing is this: Don't waste a second of your time on doubt or worry. The less fuel you give to doubt and worry, the better. That's very important. Doubt and worry weaken your concentration and create crosscurrents in the energy you are putting out.

Think about it... What is the true meaning of dedication? Dedication is a complete and total lack of doubt. Dedication is absolute devotion to your cause. Dedication is absolute faith that the universe has to deliver because this is the way the universe works.

As Deepak Chopra says in his book *Ageless Body, Timeless Mind*: "When you realize that you are held securely within this unchanging framework, the joy of free will arises. You cannot exercise free will if you fear that it will bring uncertainty, accidents, and calamity. To someone in unity, each choice is accepted within the overall pattern. If you choose A, the field will bend to accommodate you, if you choose B, the field will accommodate that, even if B is the exact opposite of A. All possibilities are acceptable to the field, since by definition the field is a state of possibilities."

So understand how your mind works—and how the universe works—and *do not doubt*. Don't let the slightest flicker of uncertainty pass across the big screen in your head that we call your mind. Not even for a second. Instead, work yourself up into a white heat of belief. Back your focus, your one-pointedness with the emotional power of your belief. Commit wholly and earnestly to whatever it is, be it person or purpose, cause or goal. Be it money, marriage, or just a new pair of shoes. Then act accordingly and consider it done...

Dedication
is the warrior's prayer
unto himself.
Stuart Wilde

Why does it work like this? Because this is the way the universe works. Nobody can explain *why*. But as I said at the beginning of this book, we human beings are starting to understand these mechanisms now and a great shift in human consciousness is taking place. Einstein's theory of relativity, the new quantum physics, the realization that matter and energy are interchangeable, have triggered a growing awareness in many people that *we are what we think we are*. And that the universe responds to our thoughts, whatever they are. Consequently, we are continually becoming what we think we are becoming. Since the universe is always reflecting our thoughts back to us, we attract into our lives whatever we dwell upon, declare, decree, and focus on.

Or as Emmet Fox said, "Like attracts like."

Or as I say, *You get what you think you're going to get.*

To Find Your Goal, Release the Old

Sounds great you say, but what if I don't know what I want to focus on. Obviously it's difficult to use your power to concentrate or focus to achieve your heart's desire if you don't know what your heart's desire is.

One good way to find out what you really want is to let go of or release what you don't want. (See Chapter 4 on The Power of Release.)

In other words, you've asked yourself: What is the mission of my life? What is my dream? What is the divine plan for my stay on Earth? And you've come up with absolute zilch.

If that's the case, if you really don't know what you want to do, achieve, be, or become, you can start cleaning up your act and creating clarity in your life by letting go of everything you are absolutely sure you don't want.

Release and let go of possessions, places, situations, people, circumstances, and relationships that no longer interest you. Just bless them with love and let them go. Create some empty space around yourself. Let some fresh air into your room, house, relationships, and life. I guarantee that interesting things will begin to happen.

Make Lists

Making lists is a very good way to clarify things for yourself. List making will help you find out what you really want. And list making is a good way to start focusing on your goals.

For starters, I suggest The Three List Technique described below. It's really quite simple, but before you start, let me remind you that you are not doing this exercise for anybody else. You are doing this exercise for *you*. Nobody else is going to read what you write, so be honest with yourself. And when you start writing, don't forget that you can always change your mind. This is an ongoing process of growth. If you write something today that you disagree with tomorrow, just change it. You can make as many lists as you like. You can rewrite them, redo them, refashion them, throw them all out, and start over every single day of the week if you want to. (This isn't a bad idea if you feel confused about your true goals.)

This exercise is meant for you. This exercise is just practice. It's strictly for your eyes only, so keep your lists secret!

The Three List Technique

1) Your Letting Go List:

Start by making a list of everything you are sure you don't want in your life. List items, people, mental conditions and attitudes, emotions, relationships, and situations at work. Don't be wishy-washy about things. Don't think about what other people might think about your Letting Go List. Just write down whatever you'd like to get rid of or release from your life. List everything that you feel is no longer for your Highest Good. It doesn't matter if the person or thing was once very important to you. Remember, releasing doesn't mean you don't like somebody or are condemning anything.

Something that once served you well can have outlived its usefulness to you. So bless it with love and let it go.

At the end of your Letting Go List, write an affirmation of release or blessing. Write something like this: I now fully and freely release all of this from my life. I bless these people and situations with love and let them go. I relax, release, and let you all go to your Highest Good.

2) Your Wishing List:

Here you should write down everything you think you would like to demonstrate in your life. Don't be afraid to list *everything* you want, your every desire. Don't write down what you think other people think you should have. Don't write down what you think other people would think is okay or acceptable for you to have or to be. This list is supposed to be what you really would like to manifest in your life. Are you sure this is all you want? Don't you want more? Don't worry about how your heart's desire compares to what you think other people want. What other people want is their business. What you want is your choice because this is your life. So don't worry about writing down things which seem totally "crazy" or hard to achieve at the moment. If you want them, write them down. As I said, this is a private list, for your own enlightenment only. This list is meant to give you something to work with, to help you focus and grow. Imagine you are a sculptor molding a piece of clay that is going to be your life. And don't forget you're not going to show this work of art (your list) to anyone. This is your secret playground. Then ask yourself: What is the real reason you're not writing down everything you really want? Is it because you're afraid you really don't deserve what you really and truly want?

Write an affirmation at the end of your list, something like this: I bless my desires with divine love and know that the universe now manifests that which is for my Highest Good. The Good of one is the Good of all.

3) Your Appreciation List:
Finally, to put all this list making into perspective and help you realize how well your life is already working, I suggest you finish this exercise by making a list of all the things in your life you feel thankful for. In other words, a list of how much the universe has already given you, the abundance that is already yours. This is an interesting exercise because once you get started, you'll find your appreciation list just keeps on growing. Just looking at this list is a sure way to make yourself feel better and happier than you did before you started. And the act of giving thanks and feeling deep appreciation has the magical power to open your heart and attract more Good into your life.

How Napoleon Hill Helped Me

When I found myself alone, a single parent with three small children to support, Napoleon Hill helped me. At the time, I had no money and no obvious way to make money. Still, I had a strong feeling that it didn't have to be that way. I felt I had the talent and ability to make money. My big problem was I didn't quite know how to proceed. I needed a concrete tool or plan to show me what practical steps to take to gain control of my life and financial affairs. I found them in one of the original, classic self-help books: *Think and Grow Rich* by Napoleon Hill.

Inspired by the rags-to-riches story of the great American multimillionaire Andrew Carnegie, Hill devoted his life to studying successful people in order to uncover the secrets behind their amazing achievements. How did these people move from often extremely humble origins and/or difficult circumstances to demonstrate such enormous success and wealth?

Think and Grow Rich presents many of their secrets and

techniques, including the role of desire, faith, persistence, planning, organizing, and such mind techniques as auto-suggestion or visualization, Master Mind groups (see Chapter 18 on The Power of Friends), and more.

Hill says in his book: "Every human being who reaches the age of understanding of the purpose of money wishes for it. *Wishing* will not bring riches. But *desiring* riches with a state of mind that becomes an obsession, then planning definite ways and means to acquire riches, and backing those plans with persistence which *does not recognize failure*, will bring riches."

Here I quote in full the Napoleon Hill exercise that got me started:

"Six Ways to Turn Desires into Gold

The method by which *desire* for riches can be transmuted into its financial equivalent consists of six definite, practical steps, viz:

First: fix in your mind the *exact* amount of money you desire. It is not sufficient merely to say, 'I want plenty of money.' Be definite as to the amount.

Second: determine exactly what you intend to *give* in return for the money you desire. (There is no such reality as 'something for nothing.')

Third: establish a definite date when you intend to *possess* the money you desire.

Fourth: create a definite plan for carrying out your desire, and begin *at once*, whether you are ready or not, to put this plan into *action*.

Fifth: write out a clear, concise statement of the amount of money you intend to acquire, name the time limit for its acquisition, state what you intend to give in return for the money, and describe clearly the plan through which you intend to accumulate it.

Sixth: read your written statement aloud, twice daily, once just before retiring at night, and once after arising in the morning. As you read—see and feel and believe yourself already in possession of the money."

I used Hill's exercise with great success for many years. From my humble starting point, I sat down and decided each year exactly how much money I wanted to make. Then I decided exactly what I was going to give in exchange for that amount of money. I then made a written statement as described above, mounted it on a piece of cardboard, and placed it by my bed. I read my statement aloud first thing every morning and last thing every evening before I went to sleep. I then closed my eyes, relaxed, and visualized my desired results in as much detail as possible. I saw myself doing the work I planned to do and receiving the fair payment I described for myself. I imagined having the money in my hands and putting it into my bank account.

Interestingly enough, every year I made *exactly* the amount of money I said I was going to make. Then every year I rewrote my statement, raised my goal, reevaluated what I was going to give in exchange for the money, and continued. And every year I reached my goal.

Whatever the mind of man
can conceive and believe
it can achieve.
Napoleon Hill

When in Doubt, Withdraw

Once you start learning to focus and using your power of concentration to achieve your goals, you will find that your power or ability varies. You will experience days, weeks, or months when your ability to focus is strong and powerful. Then suddenly, for reasons you may or may not understand, you will feel your forces are scattered and you've lost your ability to concentrate or focus.

When this happens, when you lose your focus and don't feel "right" or "strong", when you feel you've suddenly lost your sense of direction, it's always best to stop and withdraw for a while. If it's within your power, just stop and wait.

In other words, do nothing. Nothing is definitely the best cure for a sudden loss of focus. In the nothingness, in the silence, in the probably much needed moment of no significance, your focus and power will come back to you. (See Chapter 13 on The Power of Silence.)

This is because we are all so "outer" directed. When we're busy, we have a tendency to forget how the universe works. We think it's the world "out" there that is influencing us, when in fact it's not really out there at all. It's the world "in" here, inside us, that is the source of everything that's happening out there.

So remember that—and retreat, shut down, look inward when things seem diffuse, scattered, or difficult out there.

That, in fact, is what your loss of focus is telling you. It's screaming to you: Step back, step down, step aside! Get out of the way, move out of the center of attention, leave the playing field for a while, go take a cold shower, go into hiding, and look within. Find out what's going on inside of you, find out what's out of sync in your mind and/or body. Find out what you're saying, thinking, doing that's not in harmony with your purpose or goal. Find out why you're resisting. Get yourself straightened out.

And if you can, don't go out there again until your focus returns. You won't be in doubt when you are ready and able to focus again.

Ways to Practice Focusing

There are so many ways to practice focusing. I discuss other techniques in the chapters on The Power of Affirmation, The

Power of Visualization, The Power of Praise and Blessing, and The Power of Silence. In fact, you could say this whole book is about focusing techniques. So for fast results, pick the techniques that are closest to your heart and get started!

9

The Power of Secrecy

Don't give away your power by telling other people your plans, dreams, hopes, prayers, visualizations, or affirmations. And don't show other people your wheels of fortune, treasure maps, or lists.

All these techniques to gain power are for you alone.

When you reveal, share, or show, you dissipate your energy. This is because you are working on the invisible plane, on the vibrational level, where divine substance or the quantum soup is being formed, through your mind, into your reality.

Your inner work has nothing to do with other people.

Your inner work is your task.

Your inner work is your challenge.

Your inner work is yours alone.

When you speak of your dreams and plans to others, their input, comments, criticism, suggestions (no matter how loving) will rob you of your power.

So keep your plans, visualizations, notes, lists, and affirmations secret.

Talking too much about anything, not just your plans, dissipates your power too.

So keep your mouth shut as much as possible.

Keep your focus.

Actually it's much easier to stay focused when your mouth is shut.

Also, if you're confused, try to stop talking. Just keep quiet.

If you're very confused, try not to talk for a whole day and see what happens. (See Chapter 13 on The Power of Silence.) You'll be surprised how silence clears the mind.

10

The Power of Money

Most people I talk to have negative programs about money. If you take time to notice, people are always talking about money. And without being aware of it, they quickly reveal their beliefs about money and prosperity.

Most people believe in lack.

Many people believe they'll never be prosperous.

And many even believe they don't deserve to be prosperous.

Did you learn ideas like these when you were growing up: Money doesn't grow on trees. Money is the root of all evil.

If you did, do they improve the quality of your life? Do they make you happy, healthy, and prosperous?

I have noticed that it is often harder to talk to people about money, about their relationship to money, about their beliefs about money, than it is to talk about their sex lives or other so-called "personal" matters like their health or their relationship with their husbands or wives.

What Is Money?

Money is just a symbol, a symbol of energy. Money, you could say, represents the substance (matter) of our universe.

Einstein's theory of relativity demonstrated the inter-changeability of substance (matter) and energy. Scientists also tell us that there is an infinite supply of substance (matter) and energy and that there is no limit to or lack of substance or energy in this universe. If this is true, why should we lack?

Poverty Causes Misery

Money is not the source of misery, violence, crime, revolution, drug addiction or unhappiness—poverty is. If you look closely at the stories behind the bad news, you will find that poverty is almost always behind violence, crime, misery, drug addiction and unhappiness between people. I think it's pretty easy to conclude that:

Poverty is no fun.
It's hard to be happy if you are poor.
Financial problems and pressures are terribly stressful.
Financial problems and pressures often cause nervous breakdowns.
Poverty can drive people to drink and drugs.
Poverty is not only uncomfortable, it is a degrading experience.
Nobody really wants to be poor.
Normal, healthy people want to have enough money to enjoy the good things in life.

If you're honest with yourself, you'll have to admit that this is true. We all have a deep desire to enjoy the blessings and abundance of this infinite universe even though most of us have been brought up to believe that wealth is sinful. But if you recognize that we live in an abundant universe, why shouldn't we enjoy all the Good the universe has for us?

Attitudes Toward Money

Since our attitudes govern our lives, our attitudes toward money determine whether we live a life of lack or one of increasing prosperity. Do you bless your money? Do you give thanks for the blessings you already have? Do you feel you deserve abundance? If not, why not? Do you believe there is more than enough for everyone?

Focus on Prosperity

Focus on prosperity and your income will increase. Since we always manifest what we focus on, when we focus on abundance, when we feel we deserve abundance, when we joyfully accept and praise the money we have right now, we automatically attract more money.

The Law of Mind says:
Like attracts like.
Emmet Fox

Most people are using the law of attraction to do the opposite—to stay poor. Without being aware of it, they focus on and create lack in their lives by complaining about their lack of money, the high level of taxes, the high cost of living, the government, the high level of unemployment, and so forth.

Change Your Money Program

If you want to change your life, stop talking about lack. Refuse to listen to people who complain about lack. Don't participate in conversations about lack. And don't think negative thoughts about your financial situation, about the money in your bank account, or about your debts.

Instead of resenting your debts, try this. Regard every bill that drops into your mailbox as a sign that someone trusted you. They trusted you enough and believed enough in your ability to pay for these goods and services to actually give you the stuff in advance, way before you paid for it! What faith! Actually, you should bless all these bills because they are a symbol of your ability to pay for whatever you now have in your life!

Clean Up Your Act

So it's very simple. Since your money is a symbol of the abundance of the universe, it's very important to clean up your mental act in relation to money.

Don't limit yourself to a "fixed income" either. Remember, we live in an infinite universe, so abundance can come to you from many sources. Be open to new channels of supply. Be aware that your Good can come from expected and unexpected sources. Affirm daily that your Good is increasing and that it's on its way to you now. Affirm daily that you are open and receptive to a major increase in your level of prosperity right here and right now. Say yes to new Good in your life.

For example, decree for yourself:

I am open and receptive to increasing prosperity.

The universe now richly provides.

New financial channels are now opening up for me.

_____ (state the specific amount of money) comes to me now. And I accept it gladly.

Abundant supply now floods my bank account. I am open to a great increase in my financial income and give thanks for this plentiful increase now.

I give thanks for ever-increasing prosperity now. As I bless and praise my wealth, it grows.

Visualize Prosperity

You can use your power to visualize to increase your income too. Since the thoughts and mental images we consistently hold in our minds are the blueprints for life we place in our subconscious minds, whatever we picture or visualize on a consistent basis will become our reality. One of the ways to create abundance in your life is to visualize abundance on a daily basis. (For more about visualization techniques, see Chapter 6 on The Power of Visualization.)

Relax as described in Chapter 7 on The Power of Alpha,

and then visualize or see with as many details as possible the prosperity you desire.

Let's take an example. Let's say you are a real estate agent and you want to sell three houses this month. For the sale of these three houses, you are going to earn _____ (state the exact amount of money) in commission. Visualize yourself in the present tense (*right now*) successfully selling each one of these houses. Picture each house in detail, picture the people who are going to buy it, picture the exact time of the day when you are selling the house. Picture how the people look. Imagine the pleasure they feel in finding the house of their dreams. See yourself driving them back to your office and watching them sign the papers. Imagine the exact sum of the money each house is being sold for. Imagine the exact amount of your commission. See yourself collecting the money and depositing the check in your bank account. Feel the pleasure of having _____ (state exact amount) now in your bank account. Just enjoy the feeling. Then imagine how you are going to spend this money: the improvements you'll make in your life, what you will buy, where you will go, etc.

Not Too Modest or Too Wild

When doing this type of visualization exercise, it's important that you visualize what is right for you. Your pictures should not be too modest, but not too wild either in relation to your present situation. You must feel congruent or compatible with your visualizations. In other words, you must be able to mentally accept and emotionally feel good with your pictures and images, with the amount of money, and with the situations you are visualizing.

For best results, repeat this visualization exercise every day for thirty days in a row. When you are first learning this technique, it's best to stick to the same goal and keep visualizing the same result for a while. As you get more advanced and begin to see results manifesting in your life, you will be able to change your pictures more often to fit your changing needs and the different situations you find yourself in.

Act Prosperously

Once you begin to release your negative attitudes toward abundance and start changing the way you think about money, e.g. by visualizing a major leap in prosperity in your life, it's time to begin acting prosperously too.

By this I mean, if the universe is abundant, it's time to focus on the abundance you already have in your life. Don't forget, what you focus on grows. (See Chapter 8 on The Power of Focus.) So act prosperously. Wear your best clothes when you go shopping or to meetings instead of saving them for the future, even if you don't own a lot of expensive clothes.

It's important not to wait for tomorrow to enjoy the riches you already have. By enjoying feeling prosperous now, by putting your best foot forward, you attract more prosperity into your life.

It's also a good idea to enjoy the wealth you see around you, whether it is yours or not. You might want to walk through expensive shops or restaurants just to "feel" the ambiance of money. If you are going to visualize an increase in income for yourself, you must feel "comfortable" in more prosperous surroundings. Realize that the fact that other people are wealthy is just a sign that there is an abundance of wealth in the universe. You should be delighted to know that if other people can manifest prosperity in their lives, you can too.

Don't envy other people's wealth because when you feel envious, you are really affirming lack. Your envy is a sign that you don't really believe that you deserve abundance or that there is wealth enough for you.

Are You Shocked?

Many people find these new attitudes to abundance, wealth, prosperity, and money shocking when they first hear them.

Often because most of us have been brought up to believe there is something sinful about money. On closer inspection, most people are relieved when they truly understand that since we live in an infinite universe, abundance is our birthright. This also means that there is more than enough for everyone, which is important because no one wants to feel that their prosperity or gain is someone else's loss.

In the end, we realize that what we truly want is abundance and prosperity for all people on earth. And that the only sinful thing about money is the lack of it and the poverty consciousness that so many people are demonstrating in their daily lives at the moment.

11

The Power of Giving

Everything in the universe is in a state of constant flux. Nothing is static; nothing remains the same forever. In fact, the only thing that never changes is change itself.

Even though we might like to think of ourselves as solid, stable and permanent, it's only our small egos strutting about when we talk or think like this. In fact, our skin, bones, stomachs, hearts, lungs and brains are constantly disappearing into thin air to be replaced by new atoms and new cells as fast as they vanish. Our skin renews itself every month, we build a new stomach lining every five days, our liver is renewed every six weeks, and even our seemingly solid skeleton is in fact completely replaced every three months. During the course of one year, 98 percent of the atoms in our bodies are exchanged for new ones.

Yet despite this constant flux, we are eternal beings in a sea of constant change. We are symphonies of light who incarnate in bodies made up of minute, fast-moving particles of energy. There's nothing solid about us, our surroundings, or our planet.

Everything is in a state of constant flux.

Everything is changing.

And anything that resists this constant change causes problems.

All sickness
is basically congestion.
All healing
is basically circulation.

Giving Is Circulation

This is why it's so important to give. Giving is circulation, the universal cure-all. Not for the sake of others, but for our own sake.

Giving is an affirmation, a way of declaring that we understand the nature of the universe.

Give and you will receive.

Give Your Way to Health, Wealth and Happiness

People who amass, accumulate, collect, or hoard things they don't need, people who are stingy, people who are afraid of spending their money or who hide their money away in vaults and secret bank accounts, people who are possessive about their children, friends, or loved ones, are all resisting the natural order of the universe, which is *constant flow and change*.

Since we live in the midst of this massive flow of energy, since we're all just channels through which the energy flows, we can only be fine, okay, healthy, happy, prosperous, productive, and enjoy life, when we give and receive naturally. When we don't think about giving and receiving, but just do it, when we give naturally because this is the nature of life, of being okay, then we are in harmony with the universe. Circulation is the natural order of things.

In fact, when you think about it, everything is already given to us: life, air, water, our parents, our bodies, food, this planet, and people to play with. So why should we try to hold on to anything... when we already have everything? Why should we resist the flow? Of course, when we do, it's because of fear. Fear that we will lose something, fear that we won't have enough. But this fear is just an illusion. This fear springs from a basic lack of understanding of the nature of the universe. Once you remember your true origin, once you realize you already have everything, you can dissolve this fear.

So if you have any problem in your life and you want to feel better: Start giving right away! Especially when things in your life seem stuck, or when you're sick, or when you seem to lack financial means—that's when it's time to give. Giving opens up the channels again. Giving gets rid of congestion. Giving keeps the energy circulating, flowing. Giving will open the doors again so you can receive because *you must give in order to receive...* just as in Nature you must sow before you can harvest. This is the universal law. When you do not give or sow, you cannot reap.

There Are Many Ways to Give

Giving is an act of faith. Giving says you recognize that the infinite universe is the true source of all life, all abundance, and that you are a worthy child of this infinite universe who expects to receive all the blessings and abundance that the universe provides.

You can give:

Time
Money
Possessions
Praise and blessings
Love
Understanding

And you can give to:

Spiritual or religious organizations
People who give you spiritual inspiration and guidance
Organizations that work for peace or the environment
Charity, humanitarian, or cultural organizations
Other people
Yourself

Tithing

Tithing is the ancient religious practice of giving a tenth of your income to the religious and/or spiritual group, organization, or church that is providing you with spiritual inspiration and guidance. Tithing is a time-honored system and symbol of trust or faith in the God Force or Infinite Universe that provides us with all things. By giving a tenth of our income back to the source, we open the channels to receive from the source. We remove the blockages; we get things circulating again.

The mysterious prospering power of tithing is legendary. Numerous spiritual books speak of the importance of tithing. If you delve into the lives of great people and famous millionaires, you will discover that many were and are consistent tithers.

I also recommend tithing as a way of establishing spiritual calm and equilibrium in your life. When you tithe, you will feel a new sense of peacefulness. You will feel connected to the greater source of all life, and new blessings and new Good will miraculously appear in your life.

I also recommend that you keep your tithing secret. It is no one's business but your own. You are tithing for your own Highest Good and no one needs to know. (See Chapter 9 on The Power of Secrecy.) Also remember to keep your focus and tithe regularly (for example every month) and consistently to the same spiritual teacher or organization, with no strings attached as to how the money is to be used. Then trust in the universe. Trust in life. Let things circulate. Then expect the highest and best to manifest in your life.

12

The Power of Love

The Wise forever proclaim that Love is the greatest power in the Universe, the Ultimate Truth, the Divine Light. I believe it's true and you probably do too. If we believe this is true... are our lives a demonstration of this belief?

Anger Doesn't Work

We've all tried anger, and many of us are slowly learning that anger just doesn't work. Oh yes, anger might seem to work in the short run, but don't let it fool you, it's just an illusion, a short-term solution.

This is because anger, like its close relative violence, is always trying to *force* other people to do what we want them to do or what we think is best for them. If a solution is arrived at through anger or violence, you can be sure it is not for everyone's Highest Good, so it won't last. In the long run, it will crumble, fade, and disappear.

As far as I can see, you probably won't be able to give up anger as a problem-solving method until you realize that nobody, and I mean nobody, is going to come and *save you from your life*. You are going to have to do it all by yourself. And when you realize that the responsibility for your life is yours and yours alone, love becomes a serious option.

People Problems

Most of our problems in life are people problems. Just think about it for a moment. Don't most of your problems revolve around other people? Isn't it usually the people at work, or your in-laws, or your friends, or the authorities, or the other people on your street or in your neighborhood?

At the workplace, I seldom see people having serious problems with their jobs because they are bumbling idiots who don't have the skill to do the job at hand. Nine times out of ten, it's because they don't know how to get along with other people. Their problems are people problems because they're either too impatient, too unpleasant, too inconsiderate, too sloppy, or too angry to get along with others. In short, getting along with others is the key issue, not the job at hand.

The only viable solution is the problem-solving power of love.

Now by this, I don't mean mushy, sentimental, emotional, romantic, or melodramatic love.

I mean impersonal love or love without attachment, the kind of love that is eternal, infinite, and divine, the love that holds our universe together and which translates into the Highest Good for everyone involved in every situation.

You can only feel this kind of love, love without sentimental or emotional attachment, when you realize that everyone on the planet is going through the learning experiences he or she needs to further their soul development and growth. When we recognize this, we also realize it's none of our business, nor is it our job or mission, to interfere or infringe on other people's evolutionary experiences. This kind of non-attached love is all encompassing or universal. This kind of love lets other people grow and evolve in whatever ways are best for them.

Bless Them With Love

Whenever you have problems with other people, whether at home or at work, that is the time to bless both the people and the problems with love. Of course it's nice and it's easiest to bless the people you love and care for, and of course you should bless them. Obviously it's much harder to bless the people who bother you, but it should help you to know that blessing difficult, irritating people with love really works wonders too.

For example, if you are having a problem with someone at your office, try to visualize the person and the situation surrounded by the white light of divine love. (See Chapter 6 on The Power of Visualization.) Sit quietly for a few minutes and see the problem with this person being solved in a harmonious, loving manner. Surround this troublesome person/situation with love. Then bless the person/situation with love and decree aloud if you are alone: "I bless you _____ (name) with love."

You can also say the same for the situation. For example, "I bless the matter of _____ at the office with love."

Say your affirmations aloud fifteen times in a row. (See Chapter 3 on The Power of Affirmation.)

I also find that amazing things happen when I'm in an unpleasant situation if I silently bless the people involved with love, while I'm in the middle of the situation. It's as if everything changes when loving vibrations enter the situation.

Bless a thing and it will bless you.
Curse a thing and it will curse you.
Emmet Fox

Bless Everything

Not only can you bless difficult people and situations with love, you can bless everything in your life with love, from your car to your computer and washing machine to your local grocer and your monthly bills. As you do, you will notice how things begin to flow more easily for you. Life changes when you stop resisting and fighting. When you no longer curse something, but bless it with love instead, its behavior changes, even if it is a so-called inanimate object like your computer. This is, after all, an intelligent universe we live in.

Bless your life, your body, your health, your work, your problems, your food, your home, your past, your present, your childhood, your future, your teachers, your books, your music, your possessions, your tools, your friends, your enemies, your family, your partner, your children, your parents, your job, your colleagues, your car, your money, your income, your debts, your bills, your street, your neighborhood, your country, the planet, the sun, the moon, the stars, the universe... surround and bless everything with love.

How My Son Blessed the Clinic

My son was going to a special clinic for some problem he had with his feet. One day he came home from the clinic and complained that the place was more like a factory than a place of healing. He said you had to wait such a long time until it was your turn, and when finally it was your turn, the doctors didn't even have enough time to speak civilly to their patients or explain what they were doing.

I suggested that the next time he was scheduled to go, he try blessing both the doctors and the clinic with love before he went and that he visualize the clinic and the treatment the way he thought it should be. I also suggested that he bless the doctors and nurses while he was there and try to think about how these people were dedicating their lives to helping other people and how thankful we should be for their skills and service.

After his next visit, he came home and told me: "It was amazing. First of all, I didn't have to wait at all when I got there. And as I continued blessing the doctors and nurses, they were all so nice to me. Everyone smiled and was so friendly. And this time the doctor had plenty of time to explain to me in detail what he was doing and how many times he thought I would have to come back for more treatments."

Love requires no practice. Love is.
One cannot practice is-ness.
One can, however, practice the decision to love.
Emmanuel's Book:
A Manual for Living Comfortably in the Cosmos

13

The Power of Silence

Silence is food for the soul, a gift from God. Without silence, we may wither, become confused, or fail to realize our full potential.

Silence is a wonderful place where wonderful things happen... Silence is where we get in touch with our inner voice, our intuition, our deepest feelings, dreams, and desires... Silence is where we find the answers to questions that trouble us and the solutions to problems that seem insoluble.

So don't be afraid of silence. Seek it out. Because silence is your friend. Silence is a true blessing.

Unfortunately, many people fear silence because they do not realize that silence is their friend. A place of power, a magic garden, a sacred haven, where they can regroup, recharge, and revitalize their energy. So they only feel comfortable when they are surrounded by incessant activity, noise, talk, music, television, and the frantic pace of city life. When such people are not working, they're talking on the phone, making plans, watching television, meeting friends, going out, doing things. They're always busy and have forgotten the importance of maintaining a harmonious balance between activity and rest.

Often there is the mistaken idea that something is wrong with us if we're not doing something all the time. Are you like this? Do you believe you've got to be "productive", "active" all the time? If this is your program, I suggest you do yourself a big favor and let this idea go, because not only are you missing one of life's true pleasures, you are missing a God-given place of power. So please be clear about this: You are dissipating your life force and your creative energy if you never take time to renew yourself through silence.

Do you fear silence?
To fear silence is to fear yourself.

10 Minutes of Silence Daily

Try stopping, once a day, every day, in the middle of your busy-ness and activities, and take ten minutes to practice silence. You can do this at the office or at home. All you have to do is decide to do it.

Just sit still and be quiet. Don't do anything else. Allow yourself to settle down without thinking about anything special. For those few minutes, close your door and take the phone off the hook. Create an oasis of peace and quiet for yourself, and don't dwell on anything in particular. Let your mind go where it wants to go.

After ten minutes, return to your life. You will be amazed at the difference, especially if you practice short periods of silence on a daily basis. You will find that your ability to concentrate on the tasks at hand will increase. You will accomplish more with less effort.

An Afternoon or Day of Silence

One of the best treats you can give yourself is an afternoon or a day of silence. Especially out in Nature. As your soul absorbs the quietness of Nature and unwinds from the busy-ness of your everyday life, you might find yourself feeling like a junkie suffering from withdrawal symptoms. It's not always pleasant at first, but eventually you will find yourself calming down. After a while, the chatter in your brain will ebb and you will begin to breathe more deeply.

Without thinking, without questioning, the silence will begin to unfold, like a precious treasure, and reveal its secrets. It will bring you startling insights, and guide you, showing you the way in matters that have confused you. And more than anything, the silence will bring you an abundance of new life, new energy, and new creative ideas.

Don't be dismayed if the silence does not reveal its secret treasures to you on your first try. Your soul may be so used to incessant activity and chatter that it will take a while to adjust to silence. But as long as you practice silence on a regular basis, even for short periods, it will eventually open its doors to you because silence is our direct link to the God Force or Higher Intelligence that underlies and guides the universe. Silence is always available to you, always waiting to bring you solace, power, and guidance.

Creativity and Silence: Learning to Await the Small Voice Within

Silence always precedes creative endeavor.

If you watch carefully, you will discover that it's the quiet time, the empty space, before the act of creativity that gives birth to all creative endeavor and human achievement.

It's as if all thoughts and things emerge from the silence to grow and take form in our minds, first as ideas, and later as all the wondrous creations of humanity.

Sometimes the most difficult part of the creative process is that period of silence that precedes activity. This is because we often struggle unnecessarily and try to force results instead of resting in the silence and awaiting the small voice within...

14

The Power of Nature

One of the reasons we feel so much better when we are out in Nature is that we are so much closer to the Force. Sometimes we even feel we're in direct contact. Then it's the most wonderful, electrifying sensation... We feel strong, high, connected. We feel the Force pulsing through everything; we feel the flow and strength of it, moving in us and through us. Obviously it's much easier to feel this power outdoors, out in the woods or up in the mountains, because there's no noise, no town, no phones, no TVs, no egos, no rush, no violence, no cars, no man-made things or emotions to divert our attention and/or clutter up our consciousness.

Outdoors, if we slow down and are quiet for just a little while—then wham bang—we become aware of the universal presence. We know the Force is right there, with us and in us!

Keep Quiet

Of course it's fun to go walking in the woods with our friends and of course we should do it. But not all the time because when we're with friends, we tend to talk and gossip and yak the whole time. When this happens, when we bring all our emotions and incessant chatter with us to the great outdoors, it's hard for the Force to get our attention, because the Force doesn't sing or dance. The Force is just there. Timeless and always present, just beneath the surface. So we have to be silent enough, and open and receptive enough, for it to do its wonderful work in us. (See Chapter 13 on The Power of Silence.)

Power Spots

There are places out there, places on this earth that are more powerful than others. If you've ever been to a power spot, you know what I mean. A power spot overwhelms you with its clarity and beauty, with its sense of harmony, and with the feeling of power you experience when you stand on that spot. Some spots on the planet are so powerful that they work their magic for everybody. The desert around Santa Fe has this feeling and there are places in Denmark which do too.

But since we're all different, we can all have our special power spots too. I go to my power spots when I am in need of healing or to recharge and renew myself. For me, these places are truly sacred ground. As soon as I approach one of my special spots, I always feel much better. Just the memory of past harmony and healing instantly triggers a deep sense of peace and healing in my soul.

Find Your Own Power Spot

If you don't already have your own power spot, I suggest you make up your mind to find a spot that is right for you. A place in Nature that gives you this sense of power and harmony and where you can renew yourself. If you don't know how or where to begin, follow your intuition and just let your feet take you away.

Be open and receptive to the small voice within. Then, in your silent wandering, you will know when you find such a spot because you will feel so much better—healed of whatever ails you—after resting, relaxing, meditating, or just doing nothing on a natural power spot.

Move in Nature

Besides being silent, resting, relaxing, and quietly tuning in to the power of Nature, we can also increase our power by releasing, moving, exercising, singing and dancing outdoors.

If something is bothering you, you can try, for example, to release the situation and your emotions about the situation when you're alone out in the woods. Find a quiet spot or pathway and say affirmations of release aloud to the trees and the winding pathways until you feel a sense of peace. (See Chapter 3 on The Power of Affirmation.)

Say aloud, for example:

I now fully and freely release _____ (the person or situation). I bless you _____ (person, situation) and let you go from my life. All disharmony between us is now dissolved. You are completely free to go on to your Highest Good and I am completely free to go on to my Highest Good. All things are in perfect harmony between us, now and forever.

Find or create an affirmation that feels right to you and fits your problem or situation. Keep repeating your affirmation until you feel peaceful. When you feel a deep sense of peace and quiet inside, you will know your work is done. Then forget the whole matter and enjoy your forest walk!

Hug a Tree

Tree hugging is also a good grounding exercise when you're out in Nature. I have my special trees that I like to hug and when I do, I always feel better. I embrace my tree with both arms and hug away, with my feet firmly planted on the ground next to the tree's trunk. I enjoy feeling the enormous energy of the tree. As I hug away, I let myself follow the energy as it flows up from the tree's massive roots buried deep down in the ground and surges upward through the branches, reaching for the sky.

It's also good to stand with your back against the trunk of a tree and feel its energy running up and down your spine. This is a good exercise when things are stuck or stagnated in your life because it helps get your energy flowing.

See the Aura

If you want to practice seeing auras or the energy fields that surround every living thing, a tree is a good place to start. It's easy to see a tree's aura.

Pick a nice big tree, one that you intuitively know is bursting with energy. Stand a good distance from the tree so you can see the whole tree. Take a few deep breaths and relax. Look at the top of the tree, at the twelve o'clock position and notice the blue sky that surrounds the tree itself. Now move your eyes so you are looking at the one o'clock position above the tree. Then relax and let your eyes go out of focus. Now, without trying to refocus, look back out of the corner of your eyes to the twelve o'clock position. You will see that the tree is surrounded by a whitish-bluish-grayish border. This is the tree's field of energy or aura. As you get a little better at doing this, you will be able to see the aura around the whole tree. (It's best not to stand so you are looking directly into the sun.) Keep practicing and you'll find you have a natural talent for seeing auras! We all do. Then try seeing the auras of plants, flowers, animals, and people.

15

The Power of Eating Less

There is only one way to eat less. Stop thinking about food.

Most people want to eat less because they want to lose weight. Of course being nice and thin looks good, but that's not why I bring it up here.

There's more to eating less than being skinny.

The real point is this: If you eat less, you gain power.

First of all, when you eat less you think more clearly.

And second, you have more energy.

And third, when you eat less it's a whole lot easier to focus. Unless, of course, you're starving hungry all the time, but that's not what I mean by eating less.

By eating less, I mean eating less than you think you need. Most people eat much more than they need to eat and many are indulging in wild orgies of food overkill.

Not only does eating too much make you fat, it slows you down, makes you clumsy, sleepy, and dim-witted (by sending all the blood to your stomach and intestines instead of to your brain), ruins your ability to present your ideas clearly, lowers your sexual appetite, robs you of your ping, makes you dislike yourself, and does a whole lot of other things like making you susceptible to all kinds of awful health problems and diseases (like the ones caused by our modern way of life). All of which are of course much too unpleasant to mention in a book about power!

Eat Less, Live Longer

And to make matters worse, overeating also takes years off your life! (So why would anyone want to do it, you ask...) Tests on animals show that they live longer than their expected life span when they are slightly underfed all the time. But I'm not paying homage to eating less because I want to sell you a ticket to longer life. I'm bringing this up because eating less is also a Road to Power: When you're slightly underfed, it's easier to focus. (See Chapter 8 on The Power of Focus.)

That's right. If you eat less, you will find it easier to concentrate. Why do you think so many spiritual paths include the practice of fasting? It's because fasting is a fast, effective, and dramatic way to clear your brain. If you don't believe me, just try it for three days and see what happens. When you fast, you get rid of all the excess in your life, not just food, but everything. Fasting is a real quick way to get yourself back to basics.

Don't Think About Food

I spent many years of my life studying and teaching various food techniques and disciplines for health and happiness. Raising your awareness of the relationship between food and health is always a good starting point for improving the quality of your life. But unless you have a serious illness, I suggest you move beyond that stage as fast as you can master it. Once you get the basic idea about the importance of food in your life, you know things like: 1) Cut down on animal food and fat, 2) eat less white sugar, 3) eat fewer processed foods and fewer chemicals, 4) drink less alcohol and coffee, 5) quit smoking, and 6) eat more grains, vegetables, fruits and good bread, basic stuff like that... Well, once you get it, move on to the next item on your agenda.

And then don't think about food. Just forget it.

I find that not thinking about food, not focusing on it, is the best way to eat less.

Just look at people who are dieting. They are focusing so massively on food and on losing weight that it's impossible for them to do it. Because they're thinking negatively about food all the time. Oh my, what if I eat this. Oh my, look at my body. Oh my, look how terrible I look. Oh my, I'm so hungry. And all that stuff. So what they focus on increases. If you want to lose weight, forget about it. Fall in love, walk from the East Coast to the West Coast, decide to make a million this year, and I guarantee you will lose weight.

Fast and Light

The most important thing is to travel light. We talked about this before in the chapter on releasing. (See Chapter 4 on The Power of Release.) We also mentioned that the basic cause of all problems is *congestion* and that circulation is the basic cure. Well, overeating—eating more than you need to travel light—causes congestion in your mind, body and in your life.

So as you start your releasing exercises, I suggest you add food to your releasing agenda. Let it go. Release excess food from your life and your body will revive.

The trick is to concentrate on what's important in your life and forget the rest. Before you know it, you will be eating less. Every time you think of your body, love it and bless it. Praise your body all the time. Tell it how much you appreciate it for carrying you around and digesting your food and letting you see, hear, smell, and touch the world. The body responds to praise and blessing. Not to pigging out.

And keep busy.

And enjoy the pleasure of exercising. In whatever way suits you. Just do it.

I promise you that if you're busy, if you're focusing on your dreams and plans, if you're praising and blessing your body, if you're visualizing your way to the top of whatever mountain you're climbing at the moment, you'll probably forget to eat anyway. Which is great. It'll make you faster and lighter, it'll clear your brain, your eyesight will improve, your sense of smell will be renewed, you'll enjoy living in your body so much more, you'll like exercising more, and most important of all, *you'll discover how much more powerful you are.*

Okay, you might want to pop a few vitamin pills and drink some good fresh water and eat some nice clean carrots on your way, but if you're traveling fast and light, you probably won't have time for more than that.

16

The Power of Exercise

Besides being great fun, moving and exercising your body regularly is one of the fastest and most effective ways of raising your energy and becoming more powerful.

Most people know exercise is healthy. The benefits are obvious: better health, more energy and vitality, and a firmer, thinner, and better-looking body. But what lots of people forget, or don't know, is that exercise and movement also affect our mental, emotional, and spiritual states. I guess one of the best secret benefits of exercising is that when you move vigorously, your mind just kicks out.

Turn Off Your Brain for a While

Being very brainy, thinking a lot, being very intellectual about life can be a big problem for people. Not that thinking or being an intellectual is a bad thing in itself. Problems, however, arise if you allow your intellect to dominate your life to the exclusion of your emotional and spiritual nature.

In other words, you're too brainy if you think about and analyze things, life, people, and situations so much that you don't trust your intuition anymore. If you find that you aren't listening to your own inner voice, if you don't trust those inner promptings that we all have, if you disregard your own hunches and feelings because you can't explain or justify them "logically" to yourself or to others, then it's time to watch out. Thinking and analyzing this much could be a big danger in your life because it cuts you off from so much of the intuitive information that is everywhere available about yourself and other people, and about life and the nature of the universe in general.

The greatest war in life within each individual is between the intellect and the heart—where the heart is saying, "This is so" and the intellect is saying, "I don't understand, therefore I don't believe."

Emmanuel's Book:

A Manual for Living Comfortably in the Cosmos

The Gift of Movement

This is why physical exercise is such a gift. Physical exercise is a great way of making your mind relax its iron grip on your life. When you drench yourself in physical activity and sweat, and/or blast yourself with fresh air, deep breathing, and the splendor of the great outdoors, you tend to stop worrying and analyzing... at least for a while. So it's no wonder most people feel better as soon as they get their bodies moving.

And the great thing is it doesn't matter if you throw yourself in the deep blue sea for a swim or dance like a maniac with all the shades drawn in the privacy of your own home.

Another good thing is this: Exercising your body is a physical affirmation of power, joy, and abundance. We've looked at spoken and written affirmations. (See Chapter 3 on The Power of Affirmation.) Physical exercise is another type of affirmation. An affirmation in movement, you could say! Because when you exercise, when you move your body vigorously, you are also loving, blessing, praising, and enjoying your body and the gift of life you've been given.

And of course you can reinforce physical movement by saying affirmations aloud while you exercise, which is another surefire way to increase your results tenfold.

You can declare, for example:

My body is strong, healthy and powerful!
Perfect health is my one and only reality now!
Every day in every way my body is getting better and better!

A Power Workout

Here's a fun, energy-raising Power Workout I like. You can do it on its own or in combination with whatever other kind of exercise you like.

Step 1: Shake Your Booty!

Stand in a relaxed position with your feet planted firmly on the ground. Take a few deep breaths and relax. Start to gently shake and move your whole body. As you do, release and let go of whatever tension and tiredness you are feeling. As you gently move each part of your body, imagine that you are kindly waking up that part of your body. Start with your head and loosen up your neck gently, then move on to your shoulders, arms, fingers and hands, and back. Make whatever soft, gentle, pleasurable movements seem most natural. The goal is to relax and loosen up. Continue slowly all the way down to your toes. If you relax and take your time, you will find that each part of your body begins to loosen up and come alive again.

If you feel like it, gently shake your whole body one more time.

It's also great fun to do this exercise when you're lying down on the floor, flat on your back.

Step 2: Warm Up

Rub your hands together vigorously until you feel your palms getting warm. Then use your warm hands to warm and loosen your body from head to toe. Start at the top of your head, then move gently down to your face, neck, shoulders, stomach, legs, etc., all the way down to your toes. Take time to warm up your hands again whenever you feel they're getting too cold. When you discover a part of your body or a muscle that is tense or sore, you can spend a little extra time massaging that area of your body to help it loosen up and relax. You can even talk to your body as you massage it, telling it to relax and let go. (See Chapter 17 on The Power of Praise and Blessing.)

Step 3: Sing and Dance!

Now put on your favorite music and dance! Just let go and have some fun! Dance and move your body in whatever way you feel like, it doesn't have to look like anything special. Nobody should be watching you do this, so just relax and let go. You might want to dance real slow or real fast and crazy. Whatever suits your mood best is fine. When loosening up your body, follow your intuition, it will tell you how to move to get rid of all the kinks in your system. Don't forget, circulation is the goal.

Some people forget that music and song are also powerful affirmations, so choose your music carefully. Sometimes I'm surprised and disappointed when I discover that the words to a tune I like are very negative. It's disappointing because it means that if I keep listening to and singing a song like that, I will keep on repeating those negative affirmations, which isn't something I want to do.

Since music, songs, and words are working on a vibrational level and quickly enter our subconscious minds, it's a good idea to choose songs that are positive and life affirming if we want to feel better! So be careful when it comes to falling in love with a new song!

Step 4: Time to Sweat

After you've danced and warmed up your body (and mind), you might want to move on to some heart-thumping, heart-pumping exercise that really makes you sweat. If you don't have any particular favorite, try running for fifteen to twenty minutes in the nearest park or just keep on dancing.

Step 5: Cool Down

Finish your workout with some relaxed stretching. Start by lying on your back and allowing your breathing and pulse to slow down. You can put on some gentle, soothing music if you like. Take time to stretch every part of your body, especially those muscles you just used a lot. If you don't know any basic stretching exercises, I suggest you get yourself a good book with lots of illustrations or an exercise video. Or you might want to go to yoga or to a dance class to learn some good stretching exercises.

Step 6: Thank Your Body

You can finish your session by taking a good look at yourself in the mirror. Then thank your body for being so beautiful, serving you so well, being such a wonderful instrument, carrying you around all day long, digesting your food, taking you to the movies every once in a while, going for walks with you in the woods, making love to your partner, and whatever else you can think of. I guarantee you your body will glow with delight... and so will you.

Have fun!

17

The Power of Praise and Blessing

We cannot force Good into our lives.

In fact, we can never force things on the outer plane even if sometimes it seems to be that way. When it seems possible, if you observe what happens, you will find it is only temporary.

We cannot force Good into our lives, but we can make room for the Good, first by releasing negative thoughts and emotions (see Chapter 4 on The Power of Release), and second by thinking about and dwelling upon the Good. This is because we attract whatever we dwell on.

Dwell upon the Good in Others

In every interaction with other people, we are always making choices consciously or unconsciously as to what we dwell upon. We can make a conscious choice to focus on the positive in people or situations, no matter what. In other words, we can choose to concentrate on the exciting potential of the moment and of the people involved or we can allow ourselves to dwell on everything we think is "wrong" with these people and/or this situation.

On a subconscious or vibrational level, we all pick up and perceive what other people are thinking and feeling about us. We pick up their vibrations, just as they pick up ours. Then we act and respond accordingly, usually without knowing why.

Children Love Praise

Everyone knows that children flourish and grow in amazing ways when we praise them. No matter what so-called "weaknesses/defects" we may believe a child has, if we focus our attention on the child's strengths and talents, the child will flourish. The Good will grow and in the end outshine any so-called weaknesses. Why should it be any different with us, just because we're grown-up?

Focus on the Highest and Best

The most amazing things happen when you focus on the Good in people. When you meet people, even complete strangers, and you think, feel, and act according to the highest and best in them, the situation will always move toward a more positive outcome.

Even better, you can focus on the Good in others by blessing them. Say silently, *I bless you, I bless you, I bless you*, and see what happens. You'll be surprised. It's as if your positive thoughts, your focus on the highest and best in people, and your blessings for them and to them work on the invisible, vibrational level. Without knowing it, the other person feels your blessing, feels that there is no antagonism or hostility emanating from you, which makes everything flow more smoothly and easily in the situation. Your focus on the Good can change everything.

This really works because negative thoughts and feelings create resistance on the inner plane. This resistance then manifests itself as difficulties, delays, and unexpected problems on the outer plane. But by focusing on the Highest Good and using the power of praise and blessing, you can dissolve all resistance.

Bless Your Partner

While you're at it, don't forget to bless and praise your partner in life, because this can be the greatest challenge of all. We often hold grudges, dwell on minor, unimportant details, remember old hurts, and focus on weaknesses in our partners when we would laugh at and immediately overlook, dismiss or forgive the same in others.

To dissolve old hurts and resistance, affirm toward your partner: "_____ I bless you and behold you with the eyes of love."

Praise and Love Your Body

A great way to attract and manifest increased health and vitality is to dwell on how wonderful your body is.

Sit comfortably in your favorite chair or lie down on your back. Take a few minutes to relax. Then start at the top of your head and work your way slowly and lovingly down to your toes. Start at the top of your head and say things like, "I love my hair, my beautiful hair, which is strong, supple and thick. The beautiful color of my hair makes it my crowning glory." Next say, "I give thanks for my eyes, my far-seeing, beautiful green eyes with which I see and enjoy all the wonders of life..."

Continue downward and bless your nose, ears, mouth, teeth, face, neck, shoulders, and back. Find your own personal words of praise and blessing. If you don't have a lot of time, you can focus on different areas of your body. Say, for example, "I love and thank my heart, my strong, loving heart, for beating calmly, powerfully and regularly each and every day. And I bless my stomach for digesting my food so peacefully and easily..." and so forth.

Since all the universe is filled with divine intelligence, every cell of our bodies is too. As Deepak Chopra explains in his book *Ageless Body, Timeless Mind*, "The biochemistry of the body is a product of awareness. Beliefs, thoughts, and emotions create the chemical reactions that uphold life in every cell... Impulses of intelligence create your body in new forms every second. What you are is the sum total of these impulses, and by changing their patterns, you will change."

Talk to Your Body

Every cell of your body is responding to your thoughts at this very moment, whether the thoughts are negative or positive. So it might be a good idea to take a closer look at the way you think about your body right now.

Do you curse your body or bless it? If your thoughts are

not as positive as they could be, it's never too late to change. Change your thoughts about your body and watch it respond to your new thoughts and words. From this moment on decide that whenever you think of your body, or of any part of your body, you will think of it lovingly and send it positive thoughts. Decide that from now on you will always tell your body it is strong and healthy. And praise it for all it can do. Your focus on the Good will make your body thrive.

By the same token, if any part of your body is not functioning properly or is diseased (not at ease) or is causing you pain, then talk to it as you would talk to a child you love and cherish. (Do you not love and cherish your own body?) So have a nice talk with that part of your body. If you have a stomachache, have a little chat with your stomach. Say, "Dear stomach, why are you so upset today? What's the problem? Did I eat something that doesn't agree with you? Or is something eating you? Am I too tense for your liking? Am I rushing around too much? Did I drink too much coffee?" Then listen to the answers... listen to your intuition and take heed of what it says.

And don't forget to end your little conversation by saying, "Dear stomach, I really love you and bless you and thank you for the wonderful work you are doing each and every day... digesting food and emotions and ideas... you are most amazing, dear stomach. So now you can just relax. Yes, just let go and relax. Release all the pain and tension. I see every single one of your cells, dear stomach, now filled with radiant life force and shining white light. And I know that you are now feeling much, much better. Yes, right here and right now. And so it is."

Writing to the Higher Self

Writing to the Higher Self is another wonderful "praise and blessing" technique. If you are having problems with someone on the outer plane and are finding it difficult to talk to the person or reason with him or her, then try writing to the person's Higher

Self. It's a good way to bring harmony to the situation.

Since the Higher Self is the true spiritual self of every person, when you focus on a person's Higher Self, you are focusing on all that is true, good, and real about that person. Moreover, you are activating the positive energy of this soul by the focus of your attention.

I find writing to someone's Higher Self is such a very comforting thing to do when there is disharmony between you on the outer plane. Somehow, when you write to the Higher Self of someone who troubles you, you are sending your love and blessings directly to the other person's soul, bypassing their ego. This is good because the ego is the cause of so much interpersonal strife, conflict and misunderstanding.

When you write directly from your heart to another person's Higher Self, be loving and be specific. Ask the Higher Self to help manifest the Highest Good for all in the situation that is troubling you. Keep writing to this person's Higher Self every day until the situation clears up. You may be surprised at what happens. Just remember, you can never ask the Higher Self for anything less than the Highest Good for everyone involved.

You can also write to the Higher Self of your friends or loved ones when you are worried about them. For example, if someone close to you is ill or you feel they need strength and support to face a difficult challenge in their life, ask the Higher Self to guide and protect this person. Or decree: "I call upon the Higher Self of _____ to protect _____ on her way (in this situation)."

You can also write to the Higher Self of your children or to your own Higher Self. And you can call upon your own Higher Self to protect you in times of distress, just as you would call upon God, Jesus Christ, Buddha, angelic or other high spiritual beings for protection.

As with affirmations, you will gain power, strength and a sense of peace by repeating your decrees aloud many times on a daily basis, until you feel the problem has been dissolved.

18

The Power of Friends

As true friends, we can work wonders for each other.

When we are in the midst of a crisis or facing some big problem, it may seem difficult to see the Highest Good and to maintain this vision of the Highest Good, no matter what is happening on the outer plane. This happens because we are too close to the situation. We are too involved emotionally with what's happening to keep in touch with (to keep focused on) the highest, most loving universal perspective. Unfortunately, when our egos get involved in crisis or conflict like this, we may get sucked into our own fears, anxieties, resentments, doubts, and worries, especially when we are new on the Road to Power.

But a good friend can help.

A good friend is invaluable at times like this.

A good friend can make all the difference.

A good friend can turn the tide.

A good friend is a Godsend.

Everyone should have a good friend whom one can ask to speak words of truth (say positive affirmations) on one's behalf in times of crisis or when in need.

As Florence Scovel Shinn explains in her book *The Game of Life and How to Play It*, "In this instance the man could never have demonstrated alone. He needed someone to help him hold to the vision. This is what one man can do for another... The friend or 'healer' sees clearly the success, health or prosperity, and never wavers, because he is not close to the situation. It is much easier to 'demonstrate' for someone else than for one's self, so a person should not hesitate to ask for help, if he feels himself wavering."

Ask Your Friend

I strongly advise asking a close friend to speak words declaring positive results for you when you are in need. For example, when you face an unusual or difficult situation, ask your friend to affirm a successful outcome for you. (See Chapter 3 on The Power of Affirmation and Chapter 17 on The Power of Praise and Blessing.) Your friend can affirm for you:

_____ *(name), the job interview is a great success. You are relaxed and present yourself in the best possible way.*

_____ *(name), the operation is a complete success. You recover quickly and are healthier than ever before.*

_____ *(name), I know you give birth to a healthy child peacefully and easily.*

_____ *(name), you are definitely capable of this task. You have the talent to do the job. I see you going from success to success with this project.*

And obviously we can do the same for our friends. In fact, I believe we should not hesitate to speak words of power for our friends, even if they are too shy to ask for our help and even in cases when our friends don't share our view of life or realize exactly what we are doing.

Listen to your intuition and you will know when you are needed. Then dare to turn the tide for your friend by speaking bold words of success!

The Master Mind Group

You can also join forces with one or more of your friends to achieve definite goals. Napoleon Hill calls the power that is generated when like-minded people join together the power of the "Master Mind." He defines the "Master Mind" concept as: "Coordination of knowledge and effort, in a spirit of harmony, between two or more people, for the attainment of a definite purpose."

Hill suggests that if properly chosen, a group of like-minded people can become a "Master Mind" group and achieve great Good when everyone focuses their energy on the same goal. "When a group of individual brains are coordinated and function in harmony, the increased energy created through that alliance becomes available to every individual brain in the group." Of course, we all do this, often unconsciously, and many successful undertakings are the result of like-minded people working in harmony toward common goals. But when you're on the Road to Power, you can consciously use this technique and create or join a "Master Mind" group to achieve your goals.

Join Together and Affirm

In like manner, we can join together to pray for, bless, or make affirmations for others. For example, a family can join together to affirm or visualize a positive outcome for a sick relative, friend or family member. Likewise, if one person in the family is facing a difficult challenge, the whole family can join together and affirm success for the individual. Family affirmations don't have to be a big deal or take a long time. Affirmations can be said at the dinner table or at some other appropriate time when everyone is present.

Or you might want to join a prayer group. Usually prayer groups work like this: Everyone in the prayer group brings his or her prayer list to the meeting. The list can be a list of people one wishes to bless or pray for or it can be a list of positive results one wants to manifest. These prayer lists are personal and secret. Everyone keeps their lists to themselves, but everyone in the group prays or affirms together for all the people or positive results on the lists.

As with the "Master Mind" concept, when people join together to make positive affirmations, the power to manifest Good is greatly increased. So let us not hesitate to work together for the Highest Good of everyone.

19

The Power of Fast Food for the Soul

Let's admit it. You're reading this book because you want change, you want a better life—and you want it now. The title of this book caught your eye because not only do you want to reclaim your power over your life, you want to reclaim it as fast as possible.

You've experienced that feeling of "divine" discontent long enough and now you want practical tools that can help you change things. You want to know most specifically how to create the Life you know deep in your heart you should be living.

And that's just great. Because it's precisely this feeling of "divine" discontent that has driven you to search for something more, for something better. And here you sit with this book in your hands—with its techniques and insights into the way the mind works, in short with precisely the tools you need. So congratulations!

If anybody had told me just a few short years ago that the simple techniques described in this book would totally transform my life—and vastly improve it—I would have laughed and said, sure. But it just so happens that they did, which is why I know they can do the same for you.

The Way the Mind Works

The real key to change is understanding the way the mind works. And now you've got that key in your hand. Now you know that your thoughts, words, and mental pictures are creating your reality; you know that what you affirm and visualize will become your Life. You also know that you are the only thinker in your mind—so you're the only one who can decide what you are going to think and focus your attention on. And this is the key to freedom!

With this magical key in hand—and the practical techniques

described in this book—you have what it takes to totally transform your Life. And take it from me, it's easy to do!

Why Shouldn't It Be Easy?

One of the main messages of this book is that it's easy to live a healthy, happy, prosperous Life, even though we may have been programmed to believe otherwise. An unhappy, impoverished life is the result of our own ignorance; it's the result of our own negative mental patterns, the manifestation of our own thoughts, words, and focus on limitation. And since most people don't understand the way the mind works—how their thoughts and words are creating their reality—they are victims of their own negative thinking.

But once we understand the mechanism, we also understand that the good Life, the healthy Life, the productive, useful Life— the Life of unlimited vitality, love and exciting adventures—is our natural birthright. We realize we just forgot how to bring it forth. But now we know how to do it.

Do the Inner Work

There is, however, one condition. With this new knowledge in hand, we must be willing to do the inner work. We must be willing to take a closer look at our attitudes and mental programs, and be ruthlessly honest with ourselves. What are we thinking, what are our basic attitudes toward Life? What are we saying to ourselves and to other people on a regular basis? Are our thoughts and words good enough? Are they positive enough, kind enough, loving enough? Will they create the kind of Life, the kind of world, the kind of reality we really want… for ourselves and for our families, friends, and fellow human beings?

The Road to Power

So you decide.

It's up to you! You can claim your own power now. You can take control of your thoughts, words, and the focus of your attention and consciously create the Life you want to live.

The tools are right here. The way before you is wide open.

So be bold. Be brave. Take control of your destiny now. Think for yourself—and get going.

Nobody else can do it for you.

Nobody else can take it from you.

This is the Road to Power.

Book 2

1

The Road to Power

Hallelujah!

Do you realize how liberating it is! How absolutely exhilarating it is, to know that you, yes little you, no matter how sad and miserable you may be today—can change your life, can change your life so completely, so drastically, that it becomes so much better, happier, joyful and more exciting than it ever was before? So much more miraculous than you ever imagined it could be... and that this is something you can do, all by your self...

The Power of Inner Work

Now there is only one condition if you want to change your life, one very important, very crucial condition: You must be willing to do the inner work—all by yourself.

No one else can do it for you. No one else can remake your life for you. No one. Not even your guru, your therapist, your healer, your mother, your lover, your priest, your boss—or a pile of money in your bank account—can do that. In fact, there's not a person alive on the planet today who can do it for you (even though lots of people can provide help and encouragement). But they can't do it for you, not even if they wanted to.

But do not dismay! If you are fiercely determined, if you're willing to take up the challenge, all by yourself, there's no limit to the freedom, success, joy, health and happiness you can achieve. *No limit!*

When I realized this truth it changed my whole life. That's why I can promise you it will change yours, too.

You Are Free

So you see, there is no discovery you can possibly make that's more thrilling, more wonderfully exhilarating, than this one. Not even winning the lottery or finding the love of your life is better than this, because this discovery means *you're free*—now and forever. This discovery means peace of mind can be yours— now and forever. And what could be more wonderful, more exhilarating than that?

To know, to really know and deeply understand, that since you yourself created your life and reality, you yourself—and no one else—can also change your life for the better at any moment in time… this is, without doubt, the greatest discovery you'll ever make.

Just think for a moment about what this really means.

The Quest

The tools are right here before you. There are teachers, plenty of wonderful teachers everywhere. All you have to do is have a passionate, burning desire to take control, take charge and change your own life for the better and then take up the challenge! In fact, it couldn't be easier. All you have to do is decide.

But in fact it's more than just a challenge… much more. It is a great adventure, you could say it's the adventure of a lifetime— your lifetime. The most exciting adventure or quest you'll ever go on, because you can't conceive of the treasures waiting for you up ahead and because this quest is yours and yours alone.

Be Brave!

No one will ever know, no one will ever understand, exactly what your quest has been like or is like right now. Which is why this quest is not for the fainthearted. Oh no. Along the way, you will certainly meet many dragons, obstacles, and alluring traps, which is why I call it a quest. So you will have to learn to be fiercely determined. To take council with yourself, by yourself— and to be stouthearted and brave. But I know for a fact that if you've picked up this book, you've already decided, somewhere deep down inside (even if you're not yet aware of it), that you'll settle for nothing less. And why should you?

The Universe Is Yours!

The whole universe is yours! The whole universe is your classroom, your playground... Life on Planet Earth is your school right now, part of the curriculum you designed for yourself, so to speak.

So why not step right up to the head of the class and graduate to the true freedom that is waiting for you—right here and right now! You can bet your life that what our society calls "school" was never this much fun!

2

The Power of Reality

We live in a mental universe
Life is a mind game
Everyone is destined to win

This is another book about power.

This is another book about the ways in which you can control your life and create the life you've always wanted to live.

But before we continue down the Road to Power—and you learn more ways to enhance and enjoy your life—let's take a step back and look at the Nature of Reality.

The Nature of Reality

To really look reality in the eye, we have to step outside the illusion of the collective consciousness for a moment and leave the hustle and bustle of ordinary, everyday Life behind.

This ability to step outside the collective consciousness is vitally important when you're on the Road to Power because if you can't, you might get the mistaken idea that the techniques in this book—and in my first *Road to Power* book—are some kind of magic or miracle cure. But they're definitely not. Everything in this book—all the techniques, methods and exercises—work because they are based on a deep understanding of the Nature of Reality.

That is why it's so important for you to be able to step outside of the collective consciousness and understand the Nature of Reality. Unless you cultivate this ability, it will be difficult to make these techniques work for you.

The Mystics Were Right

We live in exciting times because Science—more specifically quantum physics—is proving what the Mystics and Metaphysicians throughout history have long proclaimed. We are bundles of information and energy, living in a swirling sea of infinite energy. We are in truth, Creatures of Light, as the Mystics long have described us.

Scientists have delved into the nature of matter (what we ordinary folk call reality) and found, according to quantum physics, that matter is made up of atoms which are made up of clouds of subatomic particles. These subatomic particles are actually waves of energy, which are so small that their existence has only been verified by the trails they leave behind in particle accelerators.

Probably the most interesting aspect of the quantum field is that these waves of energy only become particles (localized events in time and space) when they are observed. In other words, these waves of energy which make up the entire universe only come into existence when they are observed (as Einstein suggested at the beginning of this century). This not only means that the quantum field responds to the observer, it means that everything we call the physical world is, in fact, a response of the observer.

A Mind-Boggling Discovery

This is quite a mind-boggling discovery, isn't it? Just think about what this means: *Particles only come into existence when we pay attention to them.* In other words, human consciousness not only influences the quantum field we live in; human consciousness is actually the creator of the events that are taking place in this field. And not only that—by changing the focus of our attention, we also *change* the field of information and energy we live in. In short, the quality of our thoughts and the focus of our attention have the power to influence and organize the infinite field of information and energy we are a part of.

Now what does this mean?

Plastic to Our Thoughts

This means quite simply that we live in a universe, which is plastic to our thoughts. In other words, the universe is responsive to our thoughts, attention and intentions. You could say: *We live in a mental universe.*

If this is true, it also means that the old "materialistic" interpretation of reality, i.e. the idea that the universe was out there, outside of us, separate from us, is simply not true. There is no universe or reality "out there" which is separate from us— which is somewhere else, doing things to us like controlling our lives and determining our destinies.

Unfortunately for most people, the collective consciousness hasn't yet caught up with and digested the discoveries of modern science. But the truth of the matter is that quantum physics long ago proved that the Nature of Reality is quite different from what most people today still base their lives, their opinions... their very existence on.

In other words, if you believe that you live in a materialistic universe, which is doing things to you—if you believe there is an "objective reality" out there which is separate and independent from yourself—*you are living in an illusion.* You are making your decisions and living your life according to an obsolete and outdated worldview that is incorrect. And not only is this worldview incorrect, it does nothing to enhance your life or your reality.

In fact, this outdated and incorrect materialistic view of the universe is robbing you of your true power.

When you understand the Nature of Reality, you will see that the truth of the matter is that you have far more power than you ever dreamed of.

The truth of the matter is that we all live in a mental universe.

115

The truth of the matter is that you are a co-creator.

The truth of the matter is that *you are creating this universe as you go along.*

If you can grasp this, it will revolutionize your life.

This means that if we live in a mental universe and we learn to control our minds and direct our attention, we gain power over the so-called "outer world" and so-called "outer events."

3

The Power of the Force

To know and integrate the power of the Force in your life, I suggest the following:

Take time to observe the rhythms of the Universe.

Watch how the stars appear in the sky in their correct positions, every single night. Or if the night sky isn't clear enough for stargazing, spend an hour or two browsing through David Malin's extraordinary book, *A View of the Universe*.

Then remind yourself that the sun really does come up every morning in the east and go down every evening in the west. And that the moon appears exactly as predicted in the night sky. And that the seasons continually change so that spring arrives just when it's supposed to. With all the appropriate flourishes like flowers budding and birds migrating at precisely the right time, always returning to the very place they're supposed to return to.

Then ponder upon the millions of cells in your body. Meditate on how an amazingly complex living, breathing, thinking human being like yourself developed from a single fertilized egg. Guided and directed by nothing more (and nothing less!) than the amazingly complex information (intelligence) which is stored in the DNA.

The Universe Is Intelligent

Does this constant movement... such as the growth of a human being from a single cell—or the vast dance of the stars and galaxies—or the steady rotation of the earth on its axis as we hurtle through space... not to mention the biological rhythms of all the myriad plants and animals—does any of this astonishing and wonderful movement of energy seem to be random, haphazard or chaotic in any of its aspects?

Not in the least. In fact, the more you observe, the more you allow yourself to experience the infinite field of energy swirling in you and around you, the more you will discover that orderly patterns exist everywhere in Nature. Then it will probably dawn on you—if it hasn't already—that not only is the Universe intelligently organized, *the Universe Itself is Intelligent!*

Be Silent and Observe

I also suggest you treat yourself to some exquisite silence out in Nature (see Chapter 13 on The Power of Silence in Book 1). Give yourself time to contemplate and absorb just a small fraction of the intricacies of this magnificent dance of the Universe that is going on in us and around us all the time.

Try shorter or longer periods of silence in Nature and just observe. Besides being so much fun, being silent in Nature also makes it much easier to digest and absorb the ideas and concepts in this book.

Observe the cosmic dance—the intelligent cosmic dance—which is taking place everywhere, all around you, in every leaf and tree, in every blade of grass, in every bird and bee, in every wave of the sea and cloud in the sky, in every cell of your body.

Then Savor the Force!

Contemplate, yes contemplate!

And then savor the Force!

Let the immenseness of this dance of Infinity sink slowly into your consciousness. Watch it and absorb it, until you begin to sense, even if only faintly at first, the Force or Cosmic Intelligence which is behind everything, which is directing, coordinating, managing, arranging, organizing this infinite dance of which we all are a part.

And call this Force anything you like!

Call this Force—Cosmic Intelligence or God or Brahman or the God Force or Divine Substance or the Source. Call it whatever you like. But whatever you call it, we're talking about the First Cause which is creating/manifesting the Infinity of All Things.

The Power of the Field

One of our best teachers, Deepak Chopra, calls the universe "the unified field" or "the field of pure potentiality." Another great teacher, Emmet Fox, calls it God, Mind or Cause.

What these enlightened men say includes things like this:

Emmet Fox: "God is the religious name for the Creator of all things. Mind is the metaphysical name, and Cause is the natural science name for God. Anything that has any real existence is an idea in the One Mind; and this is the metaphysical interpretation of the universe. From the natural science point of view we may say that all creation is the result or effect of One Cause (God), and that there are no secondary causes. Now a cause cannot be known directly. It can be known only by its effect, and so the universe is the manifestation or effect of Cause or God..." (From his book *Alter Your Life.*)

Deepak Chopra: "Behind the visible garment of the universe, beyond the mirage of molecules, the *maya*—or illusions—of physicality, lies an inherently invisible, seamless matrix made up of a nothingness. This invisible nothingness silently orchestrates, instructs, guides, governs, and compels nature to express itself with infinite creativity, infinite abundance, and unfaltering exactitude into a myriad of designs and patterns and forms." (From his book *Creating Affluence.*)

Contemplate the Power of the Force

Now how do abstract ideas like this affect our daily lives? What do they mean in practical terms? How can we use them to improve the quality of our lives?

I believe it's very simple: We are all a part of this Infinite Universe and we're all interconnected. Which means, as part of this immense dance of infinity and energy, we all—each and every one of us—have access to the strength and intelligence of the Force.

It is only our small egos, which seem to separate us. It is only our illusions—the illusions/ignorance of the collective consciousness, which we have learned and accepted—that limit our true power and our access to the Force.

So read this again and again. Ponder on these things until your subconscious mind has absorbed these ideas and concepts and then ponder some more!

4

The Power of the Choice-Maker

It's a liberating discovery to find out that *you* are the Choice-Maker in your life. And to find out (realize) that Life is not doing anything *to* you and that there are no sinister/benevolent forces outside of you which are controlling your destiny. Once you make this discovery, you empower yourself to create the life you've always wanted to live.

Our power of choice
is the greatest blessing we have,
for with it comes the ability
to select the kind of mental states
we entertain and hence our experiences.
Frederick Bailes

To understand why you're the Choice-Maker, let's take a look at the way the mind works.

To simplify matters, we can divide our mind into two parts:

Conscious mind (surface mind)
Subconscious mind (deeper mind)

You think with your conscious mind. You are aware with your conscious mind, and you select or make choices with your conscious mind.

Your subconscious or unconscious mind acts upon the selections or patterns it receives from your conscious mind. Your subconscious mind is also the place where your own personal memories and experiences are registered and stored—and where the memories and patterns of the whole human race, the so-called collective consciousness, are also stored.

Your subconscious or deeper mind creates your reality based on the blueprints for behavior, which have been deposited (imprinted) there by your conscious mind. This is why to change your behavior—and thus your outer reality—you must first change the patterns you feed your subconscious mind.

The Key to the Subconscious

As the Choice-Maker, you select the thought patterns or blueprints for life that you feed your subconscious mind. This means, if you don't like the reality you are experiencing at the moment, if there's anything about your life that's not functioning properly, if you are experiencing financial lack, dis-ease, or any other type of disharmony, you must select new thought patterns for your subconscious mind. Because your outer reality is only reflecting your deepest mental patterns.

This is a great discovery!

It's a great discovery because it means you're inherently free. Free to select new thought patterns, new blueprints, and thus create a new reality for yourself!

Eternal Vigilance

The first step in changing your mental habits is to become aware of your present mental patterns. Once you start watching your patterns, you'll realize that 99% of what you think today is a repetition of what you thought yesterday. This is very interesting: *99% of what you are thinking today is a repetition of what you thought yesterday.* If you don't believe me, try observing your thoughts for a whole day. How many *completely* new thoughts did you actually have today?

And if you were thinking anxious, fearful, depressed, cynical, critical or any other negative kinds of thoughts yesterday and the day before yesterday and the day before that, your present reality will be a reflection of that mental pattern. In other words, you will be experiencing some kind of disharmony or problem, some form of sickness, weakness or failure in some area of your life as a result of these ingrown, repetitive negative thinking patterns.

This realization is an important step forward. Once you see your patterns, once you recognize your mental habits, you can change them.

But changing mental patterns demands eternal vigilance because mental patterns quickly become ingrown mental habits. And like any other habit, it takes a determined effort in the beginning to change a habit (to replace a negative thought pattern with a positive one).

First Morning Thoughts

If you want to test yourself and experience your mental patterns, make a mental note to notice your first thoughts upon waking every morning for the next 10 days. Is the first thing you think:

- Oh what a wonderful day! I'm so excited because I know something new and wonderful is going to happen to me today.
- Oh damn, there goes the alarm and I just fell asleep. I'm more tired now than when I went to bed. I don't know how I'm going to get through another day.
- Oh no, not another day at that place. I hate my job and know I'm wasting my life and my talent there.
- Oh how lucky I am to be alive! I can't wait to tell my husband (wife) how much I love him (her) and to give my kids the biggest hugs ever. I am truly blessed.

It's an interesting experience because like any other mental pattern, your first thoughts upon waking color your whole day. As you become aware of, for example, your morning pattern, you'll also notice that you think pretty much the same thing every morning when you wake up.

Change Your Morning Pattern

Changing your morning pattern can be a good way to start selecting new thoughts and new mental patterns for yourself. This is probably why Anthony Robbins developed his five famous morning questions—to help people get started on their day in the right frame of mind. You might want to give them a try!

Anthony Robbins' Five Morning Questions:
1. What am I proud of in my life?
2. What am I grateful for?
3. Who loves me and who do I love?
4. What's great about my present situation?
5. What can I do today to make my life better?

I suggest you answer these five morning questions every morning for at least 10 days until you establish a more positive morning mental pattern.

New Food for Your Subconscious Mind

But to get back to the relation between your conscious and subconscious mind: To change your life, to change your reality, you must consciously begin to select positive, loving, joyful, healthy words and thoughts and emotions (mental patterns) for your subconscious mind. Only when you've changed your deepest mental patterns or beliefs, will you begin to see changes occur in the "outer world", i.e. in your experiences and external environment.

In other words, you demonstrate your deepest beliefs. You demonstrate (manifest) the patterns that are imprinted in your subconscious mind—and not what you say you'd like to believe or what you'd like to think you believe.

This also explains why you meet people who say one thing and demonstrate another reality in their daily lives. When this is the case, you know that what they are demonstrating (how their lives are really functioning at the moment) shows what they really believe. Their lives show us what they really believe in their heart of hearts (the patterns in their subconscious minds) even though they themselves may not be aware of their own deepest mental patterns or habits!

Techniques to Reprogram the Subconscious

This is why all the techniques described in this book and in my first *Road to Power* book are designed to reprogram the subconscious mind. All the techniques make use of two things: First, the conscious selection of new mental patterns, and second, the continued repetition of the new pattern until it is accepted by the subconscious mind.

This is also why I often recommend repeating an affirmation, a treatment or visualization exercise every day for at least 30 days—because it usually takes a while to get the subconscious mind to accept new mental patterns.

Please refer to Book 1 for detailed descriptions of many good techniques for reprogramming the subconscious mind. See chapters: The Power of Affirmation (the repetition of positive statements), The Power of Visualization (mentally seeing a new reality), The Power of Praise and Blessing, The Power of Focus, The Power of NO, The Power of Release and The Power of Giving.

The Seven Day Mental Diet

In his book, *Power Through Constructive Thinking*, which he wrote in the 1930s, Emmet Fox presents "The Seven Day Mental Diet." The mental diet is probably one of the best possible ways to become aware of your mental patterns. When explaining the mental diet, Fox outlines the first basic steps you need to take to change your mental patterns and reprogram your sub-conscious mind.

Fox says, "This then is your prescription: For seven days you must not allow yourself to dwell for a single moment on any kind of negative thought. You must watch yourself for a whole week as a cat watches a mouse, and you must not under any pretense allow your mind to dwell on any thought that is not positive, constructive, optimistic, kind."

As Fox points out, this type of mental dieting is much more strenuous than any physical diet could ever be, so it is well to consider carefully what it entails before you begin. And he continues, "The whole idea is to have seven days of unbroken mental discipline in order to get the mind definitely bent in a new direction once and for all."

Negative thoughts, according to Fox, include: "… any thought of failure, disappointment, or trouble; any thought of criticism, or spite, or jealousy, or condemnation of others, or self-condemnation; any thought of sickness or accident; or, in short, any kind of limitation or pessimistic thinking. Any thought that is not positive and constructive in character, whether it concerns you yourself or anyone else, is a negative thought."

Fox goes on to explain that he realizes that we cannot control the thoughts which just seem to pop into our minds. But he says, when you're on the mental diet, the crucial factor is this: Whenever you become aware of a negative thought, you must immediately turn it out and replace it with a positive thought. You only fall off the diet (so to speak) when you *dwell* on a negative thought. In other words, if a negative thought pops into your mind and you begin to think about it or entertain it, then you've broken your mental diet and must start the seven days all over again!

Go to Work Anyway!

But you ask—must I live in a vacuum to go on the mental diet? No, not at all! It just means that when you go to work or read the newspaper or watch TV or meet people who whine and complain or who speak negatively about things, you're still on your mental diet as long as you don't mentally agree or give your approval to what they're saying. In other words, your mental diet is not affected by other people—or outside events—as long as you don't dwell on what is happening or on the negative things other people are saying. As long as you keep your own thoughts positive and constructive, you're still on the mental diet.

Not for the Fainthearted!

The seven day mental diet is not for the fainthearted. I know because I've tried it several times. But not only is it fun, it's a real eye-opener because you can't possibly attempt the mental diet without becoming painfully aware of your own negative mental patterns and habits. The mental diet is so revealing that it can be downright embarrassing. But it's also an absolutely brilliant way to discover what's going on in your own head. So I heartily recommend you try it for seven days every now and again. It can change your life. It's certainly changed mine!

The power of "the Work"

Another great technique to uncover and identify our most basic beliefs about life and the nature of reality is "the Work" of Byron Katie.

Byron Katie was an ordinary middle-aged American woman who had an amazing awakening in 1986. Out of her experience came four simple questions that she has used to help people all over the world explore their most basic beliefs about life and reality—and understand the thoughts they have that are causing them stress and making them unhappy.

According to Katie, we have so many uninvestigated thoughts and beliefs that cause so much stress and anguish in our lives. In short, Katie says that we are constantly telling ourselves stories that are not true and it is these stories that make us miserable. Reality, says Katie, is so much kinder than our stories. Also she says that we are continually fighting the way things are and arguing with reality by telling ourselves things like "It shouldn't be raining" when the reality is that *it is raining*. Of course we can see this is absurd when it comes to the weather, but what about when it comes to our interpersonal relationships? When we say for example, "My mother should understand me" and the reality is *she doesn't*! Or "My husband should be interested in spirituality," when the reality is *he isn't*! Thoughts like these are highly stressful because we are fighting the way things are. And when we fight the way things are, we always lose. Once we start to investigate our beliefs, it can be a real eye-opener because we discover that we have so many beliefs that argue with reality.

A powerful technique

Byron Katie calls her technique "inquiry" and it's based on the following four questions, which you can ask about any of the things you believe about life and the people around you. I highly recommend that you give it a try; the result can be the most profound insights and a sense of liberation from beliefs that are causing you stress and limiting your sense of freedom.

The four questions of the Work are:

1) Is it true?
2) Can you absolutely know that it's true?
3) How do you react when you believe that thought?
4) Who would you be without the thought?

And then Katie adds what she calls the "turnaround." The turnaround is the exact opposite of your original statement or belief. And here you will often discover that the opposite is just as true or truer than your original statement.

One of the interesting things about the turnaround is that it can help you find new positive affirmations for your life! Especially if your original belief is negative. For example if your original belief is *I'm not OK*, when you investigate this belief and ask yourself if you can absolutely know if it's true (question 1 & 2), you will discover that you can't absolutely know if it's true that you are not OK. You will also find that this negative belief makes you feel bad and unable to meet many situations in a relaxed and positive way (question 3). You will also discover that if you couldn't think this thought you would feel a lot better (question 4). So the obvious turnaround is *I am OK*. To really feel how the turnaround feels for you, you can try to think of three good reasons why *I am OK* is just as true or truer than your original statement *I'm not OK*. (For example, I am OK because I went to work today and did my job. I am OK because I take good care of my children. I am OK because I pay my rent on time... etc., etc.) Now you understand why I say doing the Work can give you plenty of ammunition for new positive affirmations and help you ground them in your consciousness. If after doing the Work, your new affirmation is *I am OK* you will have even more reasons to believe it than if you were just saying the affirmation without having investigated your old negative belief.

A simple tool that works

Since we know that all our thoughts—both conscious and unconscious—determine the way we experience life, it is easy to understand the great relevance of Byron Katie's Work. The four questions might seem simple, but they are a profound tool because they can help us investigate our basic beliefs and unravel the thoughts we have that are causing us anguish. The thoughts which are preventing us from experiencing our true nature, which is love and pure delight. For more information about how to use the four questions, see Byron Katie's book *Loving What Is*.

5

The Power of Mental Technology

All the techniques I write about in this book and in my first *Road to Power* book are different types of *mental technology*. Mental technology is a phrase I've coined to describe these techniques because they are mental tools you can use to create the life you've always wanted to live. In other words, mental technologies are techniques or the different ways of taking charge of your thought processes—and as a result, the manifestation process in your life.

The manifestation process is:
Thought → Word → Manifestation on the Outer Plane.

All the techniques or mental technologies I write about aim to help you learn how to align your thinking so that you think right, speak right and act right—in accordance with the Highest Good you can conceive of. By doing this, you align yourself with the unlimited power of the Universe which is Good. (See Chapter 15 for an explanation of why this is true.)

The basic mental technologies described in Book 1—affirmations and visualizations—are easy and effective ways of aligning your thought processes with the greater Good you seek to manifest in your life. For an in-depth explanation of mental technology, see "The Mental Laws" in my book *The Awakening Human Being – A Guide to the Power of Mind*.

Based on Mental Law

The reason why these techniques or mental technologies are so effective is that they are based on impersonal mental law.

Now what is a law? A law is something that it is unchanging—a law describes something that is always true regardless of when or where the event or phenomenon takes place or who is involved. In other words, a law describes how phenomena operate in every instance, regardless of the situation. The law of gravity is a good example because it is always in operation. This means it doesn't matter if you're the President of the United States or a cleaning lady—if you jump off a 10-storey building, you will hit the ground because the law doesn't take who you are into consideration. There are no exceptions to a law. Laws describe impersonal phenomena, which operate automatically, at all times, in all places, for all people.

Mental laws are the same. They describe how mental phenomena operate and they too are unchanging. The basic mental law that governs our existence on this plane is as follows:

Thought is the cause, events are the effect.

This is the basic law of cause and effect and is the most fundamental of all mental laws. It tells us that our thoughts are creating our reality and not vice versa. For a detailed description of the other mental laws that govern our lives, see my book *The Awakening Human Being – A Guide to the Power of Mind*.

If you can understand this one law and realize its significance, you have the key to transforming your life. Because you are the sole operator of this law. In other words, the law explains how and why you, as the Choice-Maker in your life, have the power to change your life. Since thought is the causative factor in the universe, by choosing your thoughts, you are choosing your life. And since you are the only thinker in your mind, you—and you alone—have all the power to direct your thoughts and create the Life you have always desired.

Until you understand this mechanism, you are in bondage to it. Once you understand the mechanism, it is the key to freedom.

The Importance of Mental Technology

Why is mental technology so important? It's important because until we understand the basis of the manifestation process—the law of cause and effect—all our efforts to improve our lives and life on Planet Earth will be in vain. Because these efforts are based on trying to change the outer, which is effect.

By using mental technologies, we are dealing with the cause. This is the key to true success.

When we realize that *thought is the key to destiny*, we understand that working for social and political change—though highly commendable—is still dealing with the effect—and not the cause. We can legislate justice on the outer plane, but when we understand the law of cause and effect, we know that right behavior is the result of right thinking. This does not mean we should not take all practical steps in the outer world to live in peace and harmony (see Chapter 17 on The Power of the Vision), but it does mean that the next step in our evolution is to understand the real nature of cause and effect.

Continuing this line of reasoning, we also understand that most so-called "New Age" or "alternative" methods are also based on changing or manipulating things in the outer world, in other words, they deal with effects and not cause. Of course it is commendable to eat a more balanced diet, to use natural remedies, to do balancing bodywork, and to work with harmonizing psychological techniques but again, these treatments still focus on the outer—on the effects, not the cause. It is an interesting turn of the inner wheel that when we take charge of our mental focus and direct it to the Highest Good—our mental state becomes one of peace and harmony. Then we automatically eat and drink in a harmonious fashion and treat each other, the Earth, and ourselves with loving kindness.

Also, all forms of looking to the outer or to others—be it the stars, the I Ching, tarot cards, your local medium, clairvoyant reader, psychic or guru—is dealing with effects and not cause.

And giving your power to others. When you understand that *thought is the key to destiny*, you will not want to depend on anyone else's interpretation of the Nature of Reality but your own!

Take a Right Premise and Stand

All this means that when you understand that mental technology is the key to change, you will realize that all you have to do is take a right premise and stand by it. By taking a right premise, I mean aligning your thoughts, words and deeds with the Nature of Reality, which is synonymous with Highest Good you can conceive of. Then all you have to do is stand by your premise, regardless of what the outer world seems to be showing you.

Just keep your focus—on Love, health, peace, harmony—and stand.

Since you know that thought is the causative factor in the Universe, it can only be a matter of time until your demonstration is made—and your new Good manifests on the outer plane.

6

The Power of Right Seeing

A great way to raise your energy, increase your power, and improve your life is to practice what I call "right seeing."

By "right seeing", I mean focusing your attention on the Good that is already present in all people and situations. When you focus on the Good that is inherent in everyone, everywhere— you bring it forth. Then wondrous things happen and it's as if you become a magician.

Your life will take on a new glow.

People will start asking you what's your secret.

See Loveliness

Take a half an hour and sit down by yourself and focus your attention on the loveliness that is all around you. When you make up your mind to do so, you will find loveliness everywhere. Be it in the vase of yellow flowers on the table next to you or in the smile on your daughter's face or in the excitement on the face of the little boy you passed in the supermarket... or in the kindness of your doctor or the helpfulness of your bank manager or your sister's unexpected warmth yesterday or the fine, fine feeling of satisfaction you experienced after the presentation you just gave... The list is endless once you begin. But it's an exercise well worth undertaking because how can you expect to savor the Good you are dreaming of—if you believe it's somewhere far, far away? If you believe it's far, far away, it will probably stay far, far away because Life has a way of becoming for us exactly what we believe it will be.

See Strength

If you feel weak or tired or in any way despondent or disappointed with yourself or with Life, I suggest you focus your attention on "seeing strength" for a week or two. I guarantee it will revive you. Here's what to do.

Again take a half an hour a day and sit down with yourself, close your eyes—and focus your attention on the strength of Life. See the strength that is everywhere present—the strength of the Universe—the strength of this thing we call Life. Go for an imaginary walk and focus your attention on the strength of Nature. See the strength of the Earth, the strength of a great tree, the strength of the ocean pounding against the shore, the strength of the wind, the rivers; look mentally at whatever brings strength to mind. Then focus on the strength in the people around you. See the vitality of your neighbors. See their energy, their aliveness—the very same aliveness that is animating you. Remind yourself how this strength feels. Let your body thrill at the thought of this strength. Feel the strength of Life pulsating through you.

For again, how can you expect to feel strong, how can you expect to experience strength if you do not allow yourself to enjoy it?

The secret is to enjoy the strength you already have—the Life that is already given to you—because what you focus on grows.

See Goodness

No matter who you are or where you are, there is untold Goodness in your Life right now. Because you have Life itself. This means that all the Goodness of the Universe is already yours. You may find this hard to believe, but that is only because you have covered your true nature and your true power with a veil. You have forgotten that you—the Choice-Maker in your Life—are endowed with the power of focus. And that by choosing the focus of your attention, you are already bringing forth from the invisible the Life you are presently living. If this Life is less than the Good you desire, it is only because you have forgotten your true power. And because you did not understand the mechanism, you may have thought that this less than perfect Life was something that was happening to you—that you were a victim. But this is not so. The life you are presently living is the life you are choosing.

Thus when you understand the mechanism, you will see that the Goodness you seek is waiting for you to choose it.

This is the secret that the Wise have long known. That the Goodness you seek is here now. But that you—and you alone—are the only one who can bring it forth in your Life. Until you do, this Goodness will lie dormant like Sleeping Beauty—awaiting your praiseful kiss to bring it to Life.

See the Wisdom

And what about intelligence? Does there seem to be a lack of intelligent behavior around you? If so, you are again seeing the outer world mirroring your inner focus back to you.

Focusing on what you may perceive as the ignorance of others is just as devastating as focusing on poverty and lack. In fact they are the same.

If this is the case with you, perhaps it is time you sit down with yourself and practice seeing the wisdom and intelligence that is everywhere present—working in and through everyone all around you right now. This type of seeing is more than just focusing on the genius of Nature, which is relatively easy to do. This is a higher focus—a higher seeing—because it means focusing on the intelligence in your neighbors and in all the people you meet. This is a focus on the wisdom they are all expressing through their daily actions and activities. If you look carefully, you will see clearly that this intelligence is there. Fully present and that it was there all along, but you—perhaps in undo haste—forgot to recognize it for what it is. Now I suggest you take the time and do so. If you feel there is a lack of intelligence around you, I suggest you sit down with yourself—for at least a half an hour a day—and focus your attention on the intelligence of all whom you meet.

Once again, to experience intelligence, you must first recognize it.

Right Seeing

Thus right seeing is the bringing forth from the invisible into beautiful manifestation the true Goodness of Life. If it is Love you wish to see, then focus on seeing the Love that everyone is expressing and that everywhere surrounds you. Again, sit down with yourself and see it in your friends, in your family, in your neighbors, in your colleagues. Is it beauty you wish to see? Then look for beauty and recognize it. Is it prosperity you feel you are lacking? Then focus your attention on the bounty that is everywhere present—both in your own Life and in the Life of others.

It is an important turn of the inner wheel to understand that a praiseful feeling towards bounty or beauty—whether you think you own it or not—is the quickest way to call forth and experience bounty and beauty in your own life.

This is because whenever you allow yourself to see rightly— Goodness springs forth at every turn. And quite soon, you will magically find Goodness everywhere.

7

The Power of the Joyful Giver

Our home, the Infinite Universe, is a myriad dance of endless affluence and abundance, a massive flow of energy which is continually circulating and changing form.

And we ourselves are dancers of light—localized force fields—in this massive, moving field of energy which is our home. The abundant nature of this massive field is also our own true nature, thus anything we do (out of fear or ignorance) to restrict, hinder or stop this overwhelming flow of energy will lead to limitation, imbalance, stagnation, difficulty, lack and/or physical and mental illness in our lives.

This is why it's so important to learn the art of giving and receiving. Since the circulation of energy is the basic Nature of the Universe, circulation is also our own basic nature.

Giving...

When you give, you circulate energy. Thus, when you give, you are in harmony with the Nature of the Universe.

There are many ways to give or circulate energy. We can give our love, we can give our services and our aid, we can give praise, we can give joy and laughter—and understanding and encouragement. We can give our blessings. We can also give material gifts or positive words, thoughts and emotions to other people—and we can also give our time or money. Some good things to remember:

Whatever you seek, give first!
Give what you seek!
Wish for others what you wish for yourself!

... and Receiving

This vast movement of energy is not, however, a one-way street. It's more like an infinite circulatory system! So we must also be ready to receive and receive graciously the abundance of the Universe, in whatever form it chooses to come to us.

This means: Don't be a surly receiver! If you've ever met a surly receiver I'm sure you know what I mean. It's such a comedown to give something to someone who is resisting your generosity!

Being a surly receiver not only blocks the flow of energy in your direction, it's a negative affirmation. Being sullen and grouchy when the Universe sprinkles Good on your doorstep is like saying you're not worthy of receiving—or that you don't feel you have the right to receive. And you're also saying in the most fundamental way that you don't understand the Nature of the Universe.

If you keep affirming your lack of understanding by being a surly receiver, this is what you're going to get! Pretty soon, presents are going to stop coming your way!

So next time something Good turns up on your doorstep—no matter how strange or unexpected—embrace it with open arms! Be it gifts of money, praise, aid, services—be it compliments, support, encouragement, new opportunities or unexpected blessings. No matter what form the energy coming in your direction takes, whenever someone wants to give you something, receive it gratefully!

Or as Emmet Fox says in his book *Alter Your Life*, "... what we are to the universe, that will the universe be to us; that what we give out, whether it be generosity or parsimony, that we shall receive back; that like attracts like; that whatsoever a man soweth, that shall he also reap; and that no man escapes the Law."

The Joyful Giver

Once we understand this law, i.e. the Nature of the Universe, once we see ourselves as a part of this universal dance, as part of this massive exchange of energy, we can't help but become joyful givers and receivers! And being a joyful giver is just as important as being a joyful receiver...

Because the Universe loves a joyful giver!

Have you ever received a gift that was given grudgingly? If you have, you know it would have been better if the person who gave you the gift hadn't given you anything at all. Because giving without joy nullifies the act of giving all together. Probably because another intrinsic aspect of the Nature of the Universe is pure joy.

Recognize and Praise the Source!

When you realize that the Universe is the sole source of everything and the sole source of all Good, you can sing Hallelujah! And when you deeply know and understand that the Infinite Universe has created everything, including you, and that you are a part of this vast and wonderful scheme of things which is absolutely and infinitely abundant—any fear you may have in relation to giving should vanish instantly! Because:

Being a joyful giver means that you know the Nature of Reality!

Being a joyful giver means you trust the Universe!

Being a joyful giver means you know who you are!

Being a joyful giver means you know you are always at home and that your home is the Infinite Universe.

Being a joyful giver means you know there's an infinity of more.

Being a joyful giver means you know you are a part of this massive flow of energy, so how can you lack?

You Can Always Give

No matter what your present situation, you can always activate the law of circulation of energy in your life and environment by giving. Because no matter what, there's always something you can give—and give joyfully.

No matter how "poor" you may perceive yourself to be, you can always find something to give. For example, you can give someone a compliment or help friends by donating a couple of hours of your time to help them. You can offer your encouragement or support for a project; you can give wild flowers you picked in a field, or you can give a friend one of your most treasured possessions… There are countless ways to set the energy of the universe in motion in your life, no matter what your situation. (See the section on tithing in Chapter 9 on The Power of Even More Money.)

So if you want to prosper, get started right away! Set things in motion by starting the activity of circulation in your life! Give and give boldly!

A lost opportunity to give
is a lost opportunity to receive.
Jon P. Speller

Giving Dissolves Stagnation

Also if you are experiencing any type of difficulty or un-happiness, or if you have a physical or mental problem, this means that something, somewhere, is stuck in your life. Once again, a great way to dissolve stagnation is by being bold and giving joyfully!

Giving—and giving boldly and joyfully—opens the channels wide and dissolves stagnation. Giving is simply one of the best and most effective ways to set the energy of the Universe in motion again.

So let the dancers dance!

And remember—always give to others what you wish to receive yourself. (And wish for others, even your so-called "enemies", that which you wish for yourself.)

Yes, this is the unchangeable law of the Universe. Giving is like sowing: To reap your Good, you must first sow.

8

The Power of No Age

How old would you be if you didn't know your age?
    Would you be 20, 17, 95 or 5?
    How old would you be...?
    And how would you act, if you didn't know your age?

If you didn't know how old you are, it would be impossible to know how you were supposed to act. After all we've all been taught to "act our age." But if you didn't know your age, you just couldn't do it.
    So what would you do?

We all know that people who are 40 or 50 or 60 aren't supposed to act like 17-year-olds. Or like 5-year-olds or like 95-year-olds. They're supposed to be "adults" and act their age.
    But what does acting your age mean when you're 40 or 50?
    Well for one, there are lots of things you could do when you were 17 that you're not supposed to be able to do when you're 40 or 50.
    Once I was at a lecture and Wayne Dyer told this story. He was out running one day with his wife (he was 55 at the time) and there was a fence up ahead and as he started to jump over it, his wife shouted, "You can't do that..." But it was too late and he jumped over the fence anyway. Afterwards his wife said, "Wayne, you can't go jumping over fences like that... you're 55." And he said, "Oh, I forgot."
    Interesting isn't it?
    How the "age" thought limits us.
    How it limits our perception of who we are and what we can do.

Aging Is a Concept

Aging is a concept, an idea that is a part of the collective consciousness. It's deeply imbedded or programmed into each of us. This is because we've been taught, shown, conditioned, badgered, bullied and brainwashed into believing that decline, decay, disease, dreariness, dread, decrepitude, downfall, doom, disaster, and finally death are our lot.

(Other vivid words we associate with aging and old age are weak, sickly, fragile, frail, infirm, feeble, decrepit, senile, ailing, invalid…)

But what in fact is aging?

Is it written in stone that decline, decay, disaster and death are the natural order of things—and the only way out of here?

What is aging?

What is it that grows old? It's not the molecules and atoms that make up the cells of our bodies that grow old, because they are constantly being replaced. In fact, more than 98% of the atoms in our bodies are replaced during the course of one year. So what is it that grows old? Who is aging?

In *Ageless Body, Timeless Mind*, Deepak Chopra says, "The decline of vigor in old age is largely the result of people *expecting* to decline; they have unwittingly implanted a self-defeating intention in the form of a strong belief, and the mind-body connection automatically carries out this intention." In fact, continues Chopra, "Your body is aging beyond your control because it has been programmed to live out the rules of that collective conditioning."

No Limits

Every time you set limits for yourself because of your age, make a mental note to release these images of limitation and replace them with positive pictures of yourself, vigorous and thriving, at every age.

One way you can reprogram yourself is by saying positive affirmations on a daily basis. Here are some affirmations I like:

Every day in every way I am getting better and better and better!

Every cell and every atom of my body is filled with Life and Light!

I AM strong and healthy. I AM! I AM! I AM!

"I am nourished by the Spirit within. Every cell in my body is filled with Light. I give thanks for radiant health and endless happiness."
Florence Scovel Shinn

This change of life is a time of soul growth and freedom into expanded Good for me. I go through all changes, easily and peacefully.

I love my body and my body loves me.

Divine order now prevails in my mind and body.

"I am young and beautiful—at every age." Louise L. Hay

I give thanks for my ever-increasing health, strength and vitality. I am enjoying radiant good health now.

For more good body affirmations, see Chapter 3 on The Power of Affirmation in Book 1.

Bless Your Body
Emmet Fox said: "Bless a thing and it will bless you. Curse a thing and it will curse you."

So remember to bless and thank your body as often as possible. Focus on the Good. Take a little time every day if possible to ponder and enjoy the miracle that your body is. Look at yourself in the mirror and see how beautiful you really are.

Thank and bless your eyes, your ears, your nose, your mouth, your lungs, your heart, your stomach, your intestines, liver, kidneys, arms, legs, feet, hands, and each and every cell and atom in your body for giving you this wonderful opportunity to play around on Planet Earth.

A good blessing is:

I bless my body as Good, Good, Good. I bless my intestines and digestion as Good, Good, Good. I bless my heart as Good, Good, Good. I bless my _____ (name the parts of your body you want to focus on) as Good, Good, Good.

What You Focus on Increases

When you focus on the Good, the Good grows. When you focus on how strong and healthy your body is, your strength and health will increase. For more details, see Chapter 17 on The Power of Praise and Blessing in Book 1.

Time to Rethink

So all in all, it's time we take a closer look at some of the latest scientific findings on health and aging—and about the mind-body connection in general—and rethink the whole matter. And reclaim our power to consciously direct our bodies.

In fact, maybe it's time we rewrite the script on aging. And maybe the same holds true for death and dying.

Near Death Experiences

From the books I've read and TV programs I've seen about near-death experiences, it seems that almost everyone who's had a near-death experience says almost the same thing. They left their bodies and passed through a tunnel of light—and were lovingly greeted at the other end by angels or their favorite grandmother or Jesus or someone they liked/loved a lot. All these people say their experience was extremely peaceful and beautiful... and that after their near-death experience, they weren't afraid of death anymore.

A little boy I saw in a documentary film on near-death experiences said when he got up there, there was an "in" door and an "out" door. When he looked in through the "in" door where he was supposed to go in, he saw his grandparents getting ready to return to Earth through the "out" door!

Releasing the Death Fear

Can you imagine what it would be like if we didn't fear death?

Can you imagine the immense sigh of relief that would pass through the collective consciousness if everybody gave up their fear of death?

Can you imagine what a relief it would be, for you personally, if you didn't fear death anymore? If you knew without a shadow of doubt that passing over to the other side was going to be great fun—a great adventure—because you are going to meet all the people you love and you're going to hang out with Angels and all the other Divine Spirits.

What if you believed that dying would be more exciting and more fun than anything else you'd ever done on the Earth Plane? Would you live your life differently? Would you be kinder? Would you take more risks? Would you be more generous? More loving? More fun to be with? Would you laugh more at your so-called difficulties? What would you do differently if you didn't fear death?

And if you had a deep realization—a very deep realization— that you are a Divine Spirit, right here and now, this very moment, who is going to live forever somewhere, in some sphere, and who chose to come to the Earth Plane and experience Life on Planet Earth in this particular body, at this particular time, to learn these particular lessons, wouldn't your perspective on death change? Wouldn't you then just view death as another transition? Another change? And wouldn't this new perspective on Life/Death, this Bigger View, make living your present life, right here and now, a lot easier, a lot more fun...

And if this is true, then why not change your mind about death and dying, right now?

It's up to you.

Don't forget you're the Choice-Maker in your Life.

If you want to change your old mental conditioning and programs about getting older and about the process of dying—and replace them with new, positive images, I suggest you start by reading *Ageless Body, Timeless Mind* by Deepak Chopra and *Life! Reflections on Your Journey* by Louise L. Hay.

Envision Your Departure

Since what we focus on grows, why don't we all start envisioning beautiful deaths for ourselves—from this very minute on?

First of all, let's release all our old fears and all the negative images we associate with death and dying (see Chapter 4 on The Power of Release in Book 1). And instead feed our subconscious minds with some new, beautiful, wondrous, peaceful mental images (see the great Law of Substitution in Chapter 12 on The Power of Joy and Laughter).

We also need new role models! Role models who will teach us how to pass over fearlessly and peacefully...!

Everyone has heard wonderful stories of people who knew when it was time for them to depart from the Earth Plane and who prepared themselves for the journey. First they sorted out all their papers and personal belongings, then they said good-bye to their friends and loved ones, and finally, without any sense of hurry or anxiety, they sat down on a chair or went to bed and passed gently over to the other side.

Why not envision the same for yourself?

Every time you find yourself thinking negative thoughts, fear thoughts, pain thoughts, sickness thoughts, gloom and doom thoughts when you think about death, replace these negative images with a beautiful vision of yourself gently and peacefully leaving your body and ascending up a magnificent tunnel of

Light and Love. And arriving joyfully at the other end to be surrounded and embraced by more Love and more Beauty and more Peace than you ever experienced on Planet Earth.

Why not... why not give it a try?

I believe that if we, the Conscious Choice-Makers, signal our minds to change, we can release our fears, see a joyful, new vision, and gently ascend when our time comes.

So have a good trip...!

9

The Power of Even More Money

All metaphysical and spiritual teachings, past and present, emphasize the fact that as children of an abundant universe, abundance is our natural birthright. All the great teachers say in essence the same thing: There is a free-flowing, all-powerful, unlimited supply of everything we can ever need or imagine in this universe. And that at every moment, this supply is awaiting our command so it can fulfill our every demand. There is only one condition: First, we, the Choice-Makers, must consciously release this supply.

To help you, the Choice-Maker, develop a prosperity consciousness and manifest abundance in your life, there are certain principles or laws of supply you can make use of. These laws or principles are disciplines, which can help us develop a prosperity consciousness and cultivate the flow of abundance in our lives. Two powerful prosperity laws—the Law of Tenfold Return and Tithing—are explained below. But first:

Step Out of Poverty Consciousness

Let's look briefly at our hang-ups about money. As I mentioned in The Power of Money (Chapter 10 in Book 1), many people have negative attitudes towards money and believe in lack. And since they are focusing on lack, they are demonstrating (manifesting) lack in their lives, every single day of the week.

If this is true of you, if you are demonstrating lack and limitation in your life, you can change all of this. But to do so, you must first release your negative attitudes, beliefs and mental patterns about money and replace them with positive attitudes and beliefs. This mental shift—from lack to abundance—is a prerequisite to changing your financial situation and all the other outer conditions in your life.

To demonstrate prosperity, you must first know and understand that abundance is the Nature of the Universe, and that as a child of the universe, abundance is your true nature, too. As Deepak Chopra says in his book *The Seven Spiritual Laws of Success*, "… when you are grounded in the knowledge of your true Self—when you really understand your true nature—you will never feel guilty, fearful, or insecure about money, or affluence, or fulfilling your desires, because you will realize that the essence of all material wealth is life energy, it is pure potentiality. And pure potentiality is your intrinsic nature."

Lifting the Collective Consciousness

Cultivating this abundance consciousness in your life is also the best way you can help eliminate the consciousness of lack and limitation that dominates the collective consciousness of the human race at the present time. Since we are all appalled at the state of poverty and misery in which so many of our fellow beings live today, it is of the utmost importance that we all make this vital shift to wealth consciousness, as soon as possible. This is because since we are all interconnected, the thoughts and mental attitudes of each individual always influence the consciousness of the human race as a whole. So remember:

The Good of One Is the Good of All
Catherine Ponder

The Law of Tenfold Return

One of the most fun and interesting prosperity principles is the Law of Tenfold Return. Many prosperous people are working the Law of Tenfold Return without being aware of it—and some, in their wisdom, are consciously working the law.

Basically the Law of Tenfold Return says as follows: You

can use part of your money as *seed money*. In other words, you can consciously plant (sow) a specific amount of money—and immediately claim your tenfold return on this amount from the Infinite.

For example, you give a gift of $10 to a friend and as you give this gift, you mentally make your claim. You say to yourself, I give this $10 and hereby claim my tenfold return from the Infinite. I now receive $100 (10 x $10). Once you have firmly made your claim, you release it, knowing that the universe is bringing you your tenfold return, probably in ways you'd never expect.

A lost opportunity to give
is a lost opportunity to receive.
Jon P. Speller

The Seed Money Formula

For those of you who'd like to try working the Law of Tenfold Return, here in full is "The Formula for Practicing Seed Money" from Jon P. Speller's book *Seed Money in Action: Working the Law of Tenfold Return*:

"The formula is very simple:
1. Plant the *seed money*. Give the amount you wish to the organization or person you wish.
2. Now you cultivate your claim. Immediately after you make your gift, and as soon as you are alone, make your tenfold claim on the Infinite in the following manner:
   I have received _____ (tenfold the exact sum given) in return, with good to all concerned. Thank you. Thank you. Thank you.
3. Repeat your formula, time and again. Say it just before you fall asleep. Say it during the night if you awaken. Say it several times the first thing in the morning. Do it enough and then relax and follow your normal routine. It is not

necessary to overwork.

4. Start your work at a modest level, high enough that your gift and your multiplied return are both important to you, so that you will do the work as outlined consciously. If you start at too high a level so that you may begin to wonder from where all the money is coming, you are liable to incur doubts. Avoid doubts or they will manifest in your results as nothingness.

5. Tell no one of your claim or work. Do it in private. You may do it silently or aloud. You may also write your claim or claims and refer to them at times, to refresh your pattern. The only work you have to do is impress the pattern on your own consciousness.

6. In the event that your multiplied claim is not returned as rapidly as you think it should be after you have made your gift and done the work on your claim to the best of your ability, continue to work with the prosperity affirmations in this book.

7. Give your gift in the spirit of complete trust. Give it boldly, happily, impulsively, full-heartedly and generously. It will return to you tenfold in the physical counterpart of those qualities."

A Powerful Tradition

In his book, Speller gives many examples of rich and famous people such as John D. Rockefeller who understood the Law of Tenfold Return and prospered immensely by using it. Apparently, throughout his entire lifetime, Rockefeller made it a practice to give generously to people and organizations. And as a symbol of the law in action, he continued throughout his life to give every person he ever met a dime. Many thought this was just the bizarre habit of a strange old man, but those in the know, knew there was more behind Rockefeller's practice than met the eye.

Among the many who have successfully practiced this law

were other great Americans such as Andrew Carnegie, Julius Rosenwald and Andrew Mellon. All of these men became great philanthropists and used their immense fortunes to benefit the lives of countless other people. (For more about the success and prosperity secrets of such people see Napoleon Hill's book *Think and Grow Rich*.)

Planting Seed Money

But to go back to the Law of Tenfold Return: Unlike tithing (see the section on tithing below), planting seed money means planting the money in advance—as a seed—and then expecting and knowing your tenfold return will come from the universe.

In effect, when you plant seed money, you are saying: *I bless my fellow beings with this gift and hereby claim my tenfold return on this gift from the Infinite.*

Practicing the Law of Tenfold Return is a good way to test your ability to demonstrate. If you really know and understand— in your heart of hearts—that we live in an infinite universe, it should be easy for you to demonstrate your tenfold return. But if you doubt, if you do not deeply understand the Nature of the Infinite, you will probably not be able to do it.

In short: To demonstrate your tenfold return, you must be able to visualize and accept totally and completely—without the slightest shred of doubt—a tenfold return on whatever amount you are giving. If you can maintain this mental image without wavering, you will demonstrate. (If you doubt, you will demonstrate your doubts, because we always demonstrate what we believe in our heart of hearts!)

Why not a Hundredfold?

Since most people can conceive of their tenfold return, most people can also demonstrate a tenfold return. But you ask, if we live in such an infinite universe, why not demonstrate a hundredfold or a thousandfold return? This is a good point, because infinity is infinity—and you can't limit infinity. So infinity is not the problem, we're the problem!

The fact of the matter is that most people have trouble in conceiving more than their tenfold return. Most of us would find it difficult to image receiving a hundredfold return... so we start to doubt and ask ourselves where this hundredfold return is going to come from! A tenfold return is easy to conceive of and believe in because all you're doing is adding a zero to whatever amount you are giving. Most of us can do this easily.

Whatever the mind of man
can conceive and believe
it can achieve.
Napoleon Hill

But the fact is, if you can really conceive of and wholeheartedly believe in your hundredfold return—without wavering, without the slightest doubt—there's no reason why the universe will not return hundredfold to you just as easily as tenfold!

To the universe, there are no big or little demonstrations!

Test Yourself!

If you want to test and develop your mental abilities, I suggest that you start by claiming your tenfold return on modest amounts. It's much better to start small and succeed. Because success generates more success—and by succeeding, you will gain more and more confidence in this powerful mental prosperity law. As you reap your tenfold return, it will help you know and understand the Nature of Reality and the nature of your true Self. And the more you recognize the Nature of Reality and your true Self, the more prosperity you will demonstrate!

All you have to do is start giving and claiming your tenfold on a regular basis. And soon, very soon, reaping your tenfold return will become one of your nice new prosperity habits!

So be bold, be a joyful giver, and watch your Good expand! (See Chapter 7 on The Power of the Joyful Giver.)

But then again, don't believe me.

Try it for yourself!

Or as John Hoshor writes in *Seed Money: The Law of Tenfold Return and How It Works*, "... it has often been said that 'The truth shall make you free.' The only truth that will make you free is the truth which you prove for yourself. If you cannot prove it in your own experience—if you cannot apply it and demonstrate it in your daily life—whatever it is, truth or not, it will not make you free."

Tithing

Tithing is another powerful ancient prosperity tradition, which is also based on the prospering power of the number 10. Tithing, however, is not the same as practicing the Law of Tenfold Return.

When you tithe, you give ten percent of the money you already have received back to the universe. The tithe is given as a token or sign of thanksgiving and trust in the abundance of the universe. In other words, unlike the Law of Tenfold Return, the tithe is a gift you make *after* the money has been received.

The prospering power of tithing is mentioned in so many spiritual books, including the Bible. If you study the lives of rich and successful people, you will find that many attribute their wealth and their financial stability to their lifelong habit of tithing.

Traditionally, the tithe is given—with no strings attached—to the person or organization that provides one with spiritual inspiration or guidance. According to numerous accounts, people who tithe are always free from financial difficulties. This is because by freely giving 10% of their income back to the Source, which provides everything, they are demonstrating their faith in the abundance of the universe. And the universe never fails to return this trust because we always demonstrate what we believe in our heart of hearts.

Thus when we tithe on a regular basis, we are demonstrating that we understand the Nature of the Universe, the Nature of Reality. In other words, when you tithe, you are saying that you know that the universe is the source of your supply. You are also saying that you know that your business—or your boss or your clients or your customers—are not the source of your supply. They are just the channels through which your supply comes to you at any given moment. But since the universe is infinite, channels of supply can change; some channels may close as other, new and unexpected channels open up. But whatever the case, your supply is always coming to you from an unlimited number of channels, expected as well as unexpected.

Since the universal supply is unlimited, no one can limit your supply except you!

Overcome Your Fear of Lack

Tithing is also an excellent way to overcome any fear of lack, limitation or poverty you may have. And in fact, tithing is highly recommended if you are experiencing any type of financial difficulty in your life. Many people find this hard to understand at first, but tithing is an excellent way to change your financial situation. This is because tithing is a demonstration of your understanding of the abundant nature of the universe—and you always demonstrate your level of understanding.

So if you are experiencing any type of lack, try tithing (giving 10%) of your present income, no matter how small this amount is. Again, by being bold and giving joyfully, you open the door to new Good in your life. (See Chapter 7 on The Power of the Joyful Giver.)

And don't wait, because as Emmet Fox explains in his essay, "The Magic of Tithing", "Some think that because they are in pressing difficulties it is impossible for them to tithe at the present time, but they propose to do so as soon as circumstances improve. This is to miss the whole point—the greater the present necessity, the greater the need for tithing, for we know that the present difficulties can only be due to one's mental attitude (probably subconscious) and that circumstances cannot improve until there is a change in the mental attitude. True spiritual tithing will be an indication that this attitude is changing, and will be followed by the desired demonstration. Tithing being on the percentage basis, the less one has, the less he gives, so the problem adjusts itself."

Catherine Ponder has a beautiful tithing affirmation:

I no longer strain and strive,
instead I tithe and thrive!

Affirmations for Prosperity

Another good way to develop your prosperity consciousness is to focus on and affirm abundance on a regular basis.

Here's a good daily affirmation from Dr. Raymond Charles Barker's *Money Is God in Action*. If you read this affirmation aloud three times a day, every day for 30 days, you will notice definite changes in your consciousness and circumstances: "Money is God's Idea of circulation. This idea, I now accept as the basis of all my financial affairs. I like money. I believe that it is God's Activity, that it is good. I use it with wisdom, I release it with joy. I send it forth without fear, for I know that under a Divine Law, it comes back to me increased and multiplied."

To help you on your way, here are more good prosperity affirmations (you can also make up your own affirmations):

"Divine substance is the one and only reality. Divine substance heals me. Divine substance prospers me. Divine substance establishes order in my life and financial affairs now."
Catherine Ponder

161

The universe now richly provides.

I AM healthy, wealthy and wise! I AM! I AM! I AM!

I AM the rich, radiant child of the universe! I AM! I AM! I AM!

I am open to all the health and all the wealth the Universe has for me now.

"The Lord is my Shepherd, I shall not want."
the 23rd Psalm

I make _____ (state exact amount) this month (year) in return for _____ (state exactly what you're going to give).

"I have a wonderful job with a wonderful pay.
I render a wonderful service in a wonderful way!"
Florence Scovel Shinn

I give thanks for a massive increase in my income now.

I give thanks for _____ (state amount you have at the moment) because I know that it is a symbol of the abundant supply of the universe. I give thanks that 10 times this amount or _____ (state amount) comes to me now.

I always have enough money to meet all my financial obligations, easily and effortlessly.

I make _____ (state exact amount) this month, easily and effortlessly.

"Everything and everybody prospers me now."
Catherine Ponder

"All financial doors are open!
All financial channels are free!
_____ (state amount) comes to me now!"
Florence Scovel Shinn

I give thanks because my bank account is filled to overflowing with
abundant supply now!

I now choose bountiful affluence and abundance for myself and all
mankind.

I am living a happy, satisfying and abundant life—and I am helping
other people live happy, satisfying and abundant lives.

These are just examples of some powerful affirmations you can use to develop a prosperity consciousness. Since it's important to imprint your subconscious mind with new mental patterns in relation to money, wealth, prosperity and abundance, prosperity affirmations are a good way to do it. Again remember that to reprogram your subconscious mind with new mental habits, it's a good idea to repeat the same affirmations for at least 30 days in a row (see Chapter 4 on The Power of the Choice-Maker).

Loving the Tax People

When you realize that the universe is the source of all your good, your relationship to money, your job, your income, your bills, your so-called financial health and stability—and even to the tax people—changes dramatically!

Not only do you stop worrying about, cursing or even caring about the tax people or your bills, you might wake up one morning and suddenly find that the tax people just don't bother you at all! In fact, once you get the hang of it, you're liable to forget about the tax people all together! Which is great since what you focus on, grows!

When you discover that you've suddenly stopped worrying about taxes and bills, you'll also realize that this is because you now have the true key to abundance in your hand. And with this true key, you now realize, understand and *know* that nothing outside of your own consciousness can limit your Good!

You're the only person in the universe who can limit your Good.

A mind-boggling concept, isn't it—especially for all of us who were brought up believing in lack! But what a relief!

This means: Your financial state of affairs is not dependent upon any outside influence. The state of your financial health is not affected by how much tax you pay, or by the high cost of living, the rate of unemployment, or by any other factors, economic trends or people besides you. The only thing that your financial health depends on is your own consciousness. This may be difficult to grasp and accept at first, but nevertheless, it is true! (For starters, how else can we explain the enormous wealth some people demonstrate in their lives, regardless of their origins or surroundings!)

My suggestion: If you want to change your situation, read the ideas presented here over and over again. Ponder on them. Give yourself time to absorb and digest them. And then watch what happens as you begin to understand, accept and practice these concepts...

The Power of Gratitude

Another very, very important prosperity secret is gratitude! When you give thanks—wholehearted thanks—for all the abundance you already have in your life, your gratitude acts like a magnet and attracts even more good into your life.

So think upon all the Good you already have in your life: The money you already have, the friends, your good health, the beautiful nature that is everywhere, your job, your dreams, your home, the food on your table, the clothes on your back, your books, your possessions, your family, the prosperous country you live in, the exciting challenges you face, all the opportunities you have at this very moment.

Once you start thinking about all the Good you already have in your life, you can go on and on. But dwelling on the Good in your life is very important because by focusing on and giving thanks for all the Good you already have, you open your heart to an abundance of more!

Finally brethren, whatsoever things are true, whatsoever things are honest, whatsoever things are just, whatsoever things are pure, whatsoever things are lovely, whatsoever things are of good report, if there be any virtue, if there be any praise, think on these things.
Philippians 4:8

10

The Power of Clear Goals

Here is a good way to achieve your goals:

Step One: List Your Goals

Make a list of your intentions or goals.

Remember to achieve anything: *The thought must come first.*

If you can't clearly state or formulate your goal, you will probably never reach it.

Practice making lists. Refine your lists. Write down your goals for next week, next month, next year. Learn to think clearly.

Step Two: Focus

Pick the goals you want to concentrate on right now.

Don't pick too many things at one time.

For this exercise, I suggest not more than two to three goals at the same time. In fact, one goal at a time is very powerful.

Focus. Remember the power of focus. (See Chapter 8 on The Power of Focus in Book 1.)

Be sure you describe your goals as clearly as possible before you start the exercise.

Step Three: Relax

Relax.

Relax deeply.

Use any relaxation or meditation technique you like.

Get yourself into the alpha state. (See Chapter 7 on The Power of Alpha in Book 1.) (Or use my guided meditation: *"The Well of Deep Peace."*)

Breathe deeply.

Relax.

Enjoy this relaxed state for some minutes without focusing on anything in particular. As thoughts enter your mind, don't get attached to them. Just let them drift by as if you were watching your thoughts pass by on a movie screen.

Step Four: Visualize

Now review in your mind the two or three goals or intentions you wrote on your list.

See each goal or situation or achievement or whatever it is you want to manifest in your life as clearly as possible in your mind. Visualize it in detail. See it. Feel it. Enjoy it. In the present tense. Right now. In as many details as possible. (See Chapter 6 on The Power of Visualization in Book 1.)

Step Five: Give Thanks

Now rejoice and give thanks.

Enjoy the feeling of accomplishment and satisfaction that the achievement and manifestation of these goals will bring to your life. Give thanks as if they had already manifested.

Enjoy this feeling. Breathe deeply a few more times and then slowly stretch your arms, open your eyes, and go back to your daily activities.

Stay Focused

For best results, do this exercise once or twice a day, every day for 5–10 minutes each time. And don't change your goals or intentions too often. I find it's best to stick to an intention until it manifests. Or until you feel you've done enough work and should let it go for a while.

Once you get the hang of it, you will probably find that you will want to do this exercise at least once a day, every day, for the rest of your life. Not just because it works, but also because it will help you clarify where you are at the present moment—and where you're going.

Of course, your goals and intentions will change as you grow and change. Just remember:

Think clearly!

Think positively!

11

The Power of Deep Peace

The secret
behind
dynamic activity
is
deep peace

Deep peace
and
dynamic activity
are the two poles
of successful living

In the Well of Deep Peace, you will find your True Self.

The Secret

Deep peace and dynamic activity are the two poles around which the lives of truly successful people revolve.

I know it's also true that you see a lot of seemingly successful people who appear to be a non-stop whirlwind of constant activity... but how long does it last? Or to put it more correctly, how long do they last? Unfortunately many of these people die of heart attacks or suffer from all sorts of unpleasant stress-related diseases and problems. Why? Because they haven't learned the secret of balance—the secret of deep peace. They haven't yet learned that deep peace is the true source and secret behind activity which is genuinely dynamic, focused, on target—and consistently successful.

Deep Peace

What do I mean by deep peace?

Deep peace is actually the Nature of our Universe. Behind the constant, magnificent act of creation, before the unmanifest becomes the manifest, there is this deep peace I've been talking about it. (See Chapter 3 on The Power of the Force.)

And once we, humble human beings that we are, get in contact with this deep peace, we not only realize our true nature, but all our activities become infused with more power than we've ever dreamed of.

Finding (Getting in Touch With) Deep Peace

It all sounds very nice, you're thinking, but how do we go about finding this state of deep peace? In fact, there are many ways. Here are some of them:

Meditation
Silence
Being in nature
Practicing non-judgment
Prayer
Sound meditation

The goal of all these practices or techniques is to quiet your inner dialogue. If you're not already aware of it, once you try any of the techniques mentioned above, you will immediately become aware of the turbulence, the incessant chatter that is going on inside your head. For many people, this discovery is quite a surprise. When they try to sit quietly, they're overwhelmed by a constant flood of thoughts, ideas, pictures and inner talk. How can one ever get this chatter to stop—and find and experience deep peace?

First of all, all of these techniques take practice. But take heart, the more you practice, the easier it gets. And pretty soon you'll have quick and easy access to the deep peace which will provide you with a strength and vision you never knew you possessed.

Meditation

Meditation is a great way to experience deep peace. And since there are many different techniques and ways to meditate, there is no reason to make it complicated or esoteric. Pick a technique that suits your needs. And if you're like me and you like Fast Food for the Soul, here are two simple meditation techniques that are very effective. (Or try my guided meditation: *The Well of Deep Peace*.) To start with, sit in a comfortable position. (You may lie down, but it's a lot easier to fall asleep if you do.) Close your eyes, breathe deeply and relax.

Sound Meditation

A good way to quiet the mind is sound meditation (to meditate on a word or sound). There are many so-called mantras or sacred sounds you can use. The OM sound is a very good sound to start with. Once you are sitting comfortably, breathe in and as you breathe out—say OOOMMMMM aloud. Let the sound vibrate throughout your whole body and consciousness. After you've said OM aloud for a little while, you can just continue to repeat the sound silently in your head. Then, just experience the silence and deep peace. Start with just a few minutes a day and extend the length of time to 15 minutes. Do this twice a day if you have time.

Instead of OM, you can also use the words "deep peace." Again, relax and start again by inhaling and exhaling and then say "deep" as you inhale and "peace" as you exhale. After a few times, you can continue saying the words silently in your head. Then let the words go and experience the silence. You may also choose other sacred words or sounds... whatever triggers a state of deep peace in you is Good.

Heart (Love) Meditation

Another good way to meditate is again sit comfortably, breathe deeply and then focus your attention on your heart area. Then imagine your heart filled with light and love—and see your heart opening so that this light and love is flowing out into every part of your body... flooding every cell, touching every corner of your being. As the sensation grows, you will feel the light and love spreading in ever-widening circles. Then visualize and feel the light and love spreading to your family, friends, associates and fellow human beings—everywhere in the world.

The Golden Gate

To inspire you to try this love meditation, here is one of my favorite passages by Emmet Fox from the chapter entitled "The Golden Gate" from his book *Power Through Constructive Thinking*:

> *There is no difficulty that enough love will not conquer; no disease that enough love will not heal; no door that enough love will not open; no gulf that enough love will not bridge; no wall that enough love will not throw down; no sin that enough love will not redeem. It makes no difference how deeply seated may be the trouble, how hopeless the outlook, how muddled the tangle, how great the mistake; a sufficient realization of love will dissolve it. If only you could love enough you would be the happiest and most powerful being in the world.*

Deep Peace Cures Dis-ease

Experiencing deep peace on a daily basis is a good way to cure yourself of discomforts and dis-ease. Because in fact, when you think about the place in your body where you are experiencing pain or discomfort (for example, your sore throat, your stomachache), this is just a small island of discomfort in a huge ocean of comfort (which is your whole body). In other words, in relation to who you really are (and don't forget your true nature is universal), your pain or dis-ease is a small island of discomfort in an ocean of ease or comfort. As Deepak Chopra explains in his book, *Quantum Healing*, "... in comparison to any one disease, your healthy awareness is as big as an ocean."

So if you are experiencing pain or discomfort anywhere in your body, you can expand your deep peace meditation by envisioning an ocean of deep peace, an ocean of ease and comfort surrounding, flooding, overwhelming, drowning and dissolving the island of discomfort you are experiencing. Simply see and feel this island being washed away by this overwhelming ocean of deep peace, ease and comfort which is your true Self.

Silence and Nature

Another good way to contact and experience deep peace is to practice silence. And the combination of silence and Nature is always a miracle worker.

This is because when we're out in Nature, especially in places where other people seldom go, we remove ourselves from the collective consciousness. We get away from the incessant chatter that's going on all the time, in all the minds of all the other people in the entire human race. Of course it's nice to be quiet in your own home, especially if everyone else has gone out, but often there is simply too much distraction when you're at home. The other thing about being out in Nature is that most people can feel or contact the Force more easily when they're not distracted by the consciousness of other people. (See Chapter 13 on The Power of Silence in Book 1.)

There are fantastic places on the Planet where the energy or Force is especially strong. Make it a point to find and go to these power spots. (For more about power spots see Chapter 14 on The Power of Nature in Book 1.) Power spots are good places to practice silence and experience deep peace. Power spots are genuine shortcuts to getting in touch with your True Self which is deep peace.

12

The Power of Joy and Laughter

Exaltation is a magnet for all Good.
Exaltation is a magnet for all Good.
Exaltation is a magnet for all Good.
Exaltation is a magnet for all Good.
Exaltation is a magnet for all Good.

Once you've metabolized this concept, once your subconscious mind gets it, you won't ever need anything else.

Joy and laughter, exaltation (elation, exhilaration, rapture, excitement, bliss) are states of mind which attract every Good thing in this universe.

If you don't believe it, try this: Make a mental note of when Good things happen to you and you will discover they happen when you're in an elevated state of mind. And extraordinary things happen when you're in a joyful or exalted state of mind—or in love...

If you still don't believe me... just notice when the phone rings, for starters. There are no coincidences. When you're down in the dumps, the complainers never fail to call. But as soon as your mood picks up, somebody happy calls to tell you some good news.

Now why is it like this?

Because like attracts like and Life is a Mind Game.

If you really are able to grasp this, then you'll understand why exaltation is a magnet for all Good. Since like attracts like, your present situation always reflects your present state of mind.

Keep On the Beam

Which makes it all very simple. It means that to have a wonderful life, to be a great success at whatever you're doing whether it's washing windows, selling toothbrushes, writing advertising copy or managing a mega-company, all you've got to do is keep on the beam. And by keeping on the beam, I mean all you've got to do is keep your mental energy high.

And as I said, high states of mental energy include the praiseful, exalted and grateful state of mind plus all the other states just mentioned like joy and laughter... and of course love and kindness, compassion, delight and happiness. In short: All of the wonderful deep feelings and emotions that make living a joy.

Compared to keeping your mental energy high, everything else is of minor importance.

The Law of Substitution

The great Law of Substitution can help you keep your mental energy high.

Since you are the Choice-Maker (see Chapter 4 on The Power of the Choice-Maker), whenever you find yourself thinking thoughts that lower your energy (for example thoughts that are sad, critical, angry, negative, depressing or fearful), replace these low-energy thoughts immediately with positive thoughts. (See the Seven Day Mental Diet in Chapter 4 on The Power of the Choice-Maker.)

The reason the Law of Substitution works is that it's impossible to tell yourself to stop thinking negative thoughts. You just can't do it. This is because the mind doesn't work that way. The mind always has to have something to chew on. And if you say to yourself I don't want to think about this negative thing, for example, I don't want to think about how mad I am at Susan, what you're really doing is thinking even more about how mad you are at Susan. So saying to yourself I don't want to think about this matter only magnifies (focuses more energy on) your negative mental state.

The only way you can get rid of your negative thoughts about Susan (or about anything else) is to think about something else, about something completely different. This means as soon as you catch yourself thinking negatively, you must switch as fast as possible to another thought. In other words, substitute another thought for the negative thought as fast as you can.

Do Whatever It Takes!

Think about the great fun you had at the beach with your Aunt Mathilde when you were seven years old. Think about how nice you're going to look in that new dress you're going to buy tomorrow. Watch your favorite episode of *Fawlty Towers*, read an uplifting book, read Tolkien, call a friend who'll cheer you up—but do something, do anything to substitute a positive thought, a bright happy mental picture, for the negative one that's bothering you.

If your state of mind is really negative and you are having difficulty substituting positive thoughts for your negative ones, be active. Go for a long, heart-thumping run, go out dancing, go cycling, or take a swim in the ice cold sea. In short: Do whatever it takes to relax, forget and shift your focus from whatever is bringing your energy down.

Is This Brainwashing?

People sometimes ask me: Is this brainwashing?

And I say: Yes of course it is!

And I also say: If you don't control your mind, if you're not the Choice-Maker in your life, someone else is sure to be.

Our subconscious minds are picking up messages, are being programmed, all the time, every minute of the day—and have been since the moment we were born.

We have all been brainwashed (programmed) by our parents,

by our families, by our society and school and our peers and the media and television. There isn't a person alive on the planet today who hasn't been subjected to massive amounts of brainwashing. And just because society calls it "education", doesn't mean it's not brainwashing.

So I figure that if anybody's going to wash my brain, it better be me!

13

The Power of the Mental Hug

We all know how nice it is to hug and be hugged.

A great, good hug—the kind you give or get with outspread arms and great warmth and love in your heart—makes everyone feel good!

When you hug somebody, they blossom and thrive.
When somebody hugs you, you blossom and thrive.

When you hug your kids, they blossom and thrive.
When you hug your friends, they blossom and thrive.
When you hug the people you love, they blossom and thrive.

When you hug people you don't know that well,
they often become your friends.
When you hug people who trouble you,
they often become your friends.

BB's Supreme Hug Technique

I've discovered we can work on our hugs! We can become better huggers and improve the quality of our lives and our relationships by hugging more!

Here's my **Supreme Hug Technique**:

1. Position yourself at the right distance from the person you're going to hug. Not too close and not too far away!
2. Look the person straight in the eye.
3. Tilt your head to one side (very important).
4. Smile warmly, from your heart.
5. Open your arms wide.

6. With your head tilted and your arms wide open, step towards the person...

7. And then hug away!

When you get to be really good at hugging, you might want to add a little flourish to your hugging and rock back and forth a bit as you hug...!

BB's Mental Hug Technique

I've also discovered that you can hug people when you're not with them—by hugging them mentally.

Actually, I stumbled on this technique quite by accident. I was reviewing a situation in my mind that was troubling me. I was thinking about this person who I wasn't feeling comfortable with and I was trying to visualize how I could bring peace and harmony to our relationship.

In my mind, I visualized myself hugging this person. I went through the whole Supreme Hug Technique of looking the person in the eye, tilting my head to one side, smiling warmly, opening my arms wide and then hugging away. To my great surprise, not only did I feel much better immediately (I could feel that somehow I had opened for the flow of love and understanding between us), next time we met, our relationship had improved and was much more harmonious.

Since then, I often practice hugging people mentally. (See Chapter 6 on The Power of Visualization in Book 1.) I use this mental hug visualization technique both to bless the people I love who I'm not with—and to improve my relationships with people who I feel troubled about.

No Limits Hugging

The other great thing about the mental hug is that you can use it to hug people you normally wouldn't hug in real life. Either because it's someone it would be improper for you to hug (like hugging the people you meet at a business meeting or at a reception—or like hugging your bank manager!) or because it's someone you're having a hard time communicating with.

In cases where there is some kind of tension or misunderstanding between you and someone else, I suggest you give this *anyone, anywhere, anytime* mental hug technique a try. Mental hugging has a way of bypassing your mind, softening your heart, and helping bring harmony to the situation. All you have to do is give the person a warm, genuine mental hug when you are alone and relaxed. Close your eyes and visualize yourself hugging the person. And keep repeating the exercise until the situation improves.

This type of visualization has the same kind of harmonizing effect on our relationships with others as the Angel-writing technique I described in Chapter 17 in The Power of Praise and Blessing in Book 1 (Writing to the Higher Self). Problems on the outer plane often dissolve easily and peacefully when we work with love on the inner plane.

Salute the Divinity

Mental hugging, of course, is a good way of blessing other people. When we dwell on the highest and best in others, our relationships prosper and grow. (See Chapter 17 on The Power of Praise and Blessing in Book 1.)

When we give love, we receive love in return.

When we give warmth and joy, we receive warmth and joy in return.

Here's another good technique I found in Marianne Williamson's book *Illuminata*. She writes: "Look around you while you are in public somewhere or gathered with loved ones. Look into the faces of the people you see, and silently say: 'The light of God in me salutes the light of God in you.' Do it for five minutes, minimum. I defy you to do this each day for at least five minutes and *not* be happy."

14

The Power of Treatment

Treatment is definite, specific activity of mind, which verily improves conditions, changes situations and cures difficulties. Treatment is a movement of mind that has a definite beginning and end.

To give a treatment is to know the
Truth about the Nature of Reality.

When you give a "treatment", your goal is to reach a point where you know or realize the Truth about the condition, situation, difficulty or problem you are treating. To treat successfully, it is vitally important to have complete faith in your power to treat.

What Is Treatment?

Treatment, as I said, is a specific movement of mind. It is a form of mental activity and is not the same as meditation, which usually aims to quiet the mind by going beyond mental activity to a place beyond words or thoughts.

Treatment is an active mental process involving clear lines of reasoning in which you consciously direct your thoughts towards the Truth.

A Long Tradition

Treatment is not something I invented. Mental treatment is described in detail in Eastern and Western metaphysical teachings and literature. The Bible tells how Jesus healed the sick and manifested the loaves and the fishes by "treating", i.e. dwelling on the Nature of Reality. The most systematic, modern descriptions of treatment can be found in books by Western metaphysical teachers such as Emmet Fox and Science of Mind teachers like Ernest Holmes and Emma Curtis Hopkins. There are also many exciting descriptions in their books of the results people have achieved by mental treatment.

The Truth About the Nature of Reality

The truth about the Nature of Reality is that the ONE Life behind all of Creation is unlimited Life, unlimited Love, and unlimited Intelligence—in short, the Nature of Reality is Good. (See Chapter 15 on The Power of the Good for an explanation of this concept.)

Problems and difficulties arise when we are not thinking and living in harmony with the Nature of Reality. In other words, when our thoughts are incorrect or limiting—and thus prevent the full expression of the ONE Life in our lives.

Thought, as we know, is the causative factor in the Universe. This is why when our thoughts are limiting, our experiences are also limiting.

This might sound like rather abstract, but in fact when you understand the mechanism, it couldn't be simpler. The mechanism as you know is:

Thought is the key to destiny.

This means that regardless of your problem—to heal the situation, all you need to do is control your thoughts. Treatment is a form of disciplined thinking in which you look away from your problem and focus your attention on the Truth about the Nature of Reality.

Forget Your Problem!

When you do this, when you look away from or forget your problem and focus instead upon the Nature of Reality, surprising things happen. The ONE Life Force or the Great Creative Power of the Universe takes care of the details and your problem disappears. (See Chapter 3 on The Power of the Force.)

This happens because the Nature of Reality is Life, Love and Intelligence. In other words: The True Nature of the Universe is *Good*. Thus when you release your limiting thoughts about Life so that they no longer block the flow of Life, then the ONE Life or the Great Creative Power of the Universe is free to work in and through you.

Treatment Changes Things

So you see, treatment really does change things. This means that you can change your life by changing your thoughts about any difficulty you face. Since we live in a mental universe, outer conditions reflect our present thoughts and beliefs about the Nature of Reality. (See my book *The Awakening Human Being – A Guide to the Power of Mind* for a detailed explanation.)

As a result, when you dwell on a problem or on sickness, lack of supply, or on any other difficulty, your problem, sickness or lack will increase. When you withdraw your attention from your problem, it will simply disappear from lack of attention.

This is why treatment consists of stating, affirming, visualizing and knowing the Truth about a situation until it manifests in the outer world. In other words, you affirm, visualize and know the Truth about the Nature of Reality, even if it does not "appear" to be so in the outer world at the moment you are treating.

When you really understand the Nature of Reality and see the ONE Eternal, Infinite Life Force shining brightly wherever the trouble, sickness or problem appears to be... When you really see the Divine in the place, person or situation where your so-called "problem" exists... then and only then will conditions in the outer world change. In other words, your "demonstration" will come—and you will see and experience in the outer world what you realize, believe and experience on the inner plane.

You always demonstrate what you believe.

How to Treat

You can treat when you are by yourself—or you can give a treatment when you are with other people. You can also treat by yourself or with others for someone who is not present.

Let us start with treating on your own.

Treating On Your Own

Go somewhere where you can be alone and where no one will disturb you. A treatment can take anywhere from five minutes to 20 minutes or longer. You will know when you've spent enough time treating because you will probably feel a sense of peace as your realization sinks into your subconscious mind.

Before you actually begin, decide what you are going to treat for. You may want to treat one situation or problem or you might want to treat for several things.

Let us take an example. You have been feeling tired lately so you want to treat yourself for perfect health, strength and vitality.

Start With the Universe

Now that you are clear as to what you want to treat for, you are ready to begin. Sit in a comfortable position. Close your eyes. Relax and breathe deeply.

Begin your treatment by focusing your attention on the ONE Life that is the source and substance of all creation. Realize that the ONE Life creates, animates and sustains all of Life—and that this ONE Life is Good. (See Chapter 15 for an explanation.)

Next spend a few minutes going over about some of the aspects of the ONE such as Life, Love and Intelligence. Start, for example, with Life—Livingness itself—and say to yourself there is only ONE Life or ONE Force behind all of Creation—and that we are all a part of this ONE Life. And that this ONE Life is your Life. Think about how this ONE Life or Force has given you Life. And think about how this same ONE Life or Force has given Life to all people and animals and plants and to the whole Universe.

Feel how this Life—which is the very beingness of your being—is flowing in and through you right now.

Then think about Love, about the Divine Love that is behind all of Creation. Think of some of the aspects you associate with Divine Love—that it is unconditional support, unconditional comfort, unconditional understanding, unlimited protection. That it is the unlimited givingness of Life itself. Then see how this Infinite Love is flowing in and through everything and everyone. Through you, through your life, your body, your daily affairs, your friends, your family, your neighbors, all your fellow human beings—and through all of Creation. Think about how the whole of Creation and everything we experience is the Gift of the Universe to us. And that this Gift of Life is in fact what Divine Love is.

Next think about the vast, amazing Cosmic Intelligence that is behind all of Creation and how it directs, coordinates, guides and organizes all Life and the infinite Creativity of which we all are a part. Realize that this Intelligence is working in and through you—and is in fact what you are. (For more inspiration see Chapter 3 on The Power of the Force.)

Stay Relaxed

Do this in a very relaxed manner. Don't force anything, just dwell on the Nature of Reality for a while and let some of these ideas permeate your being. When you've spent a few minutes doing this and feel relaxed, claim that the ONE Life Force or the Great Creative Power of the Universe is now working in and through you.

Feel how this all-powerful ONE Life Force that created all of Creation is giving you Life and animating and vitalizing every cell, every muscle and every organ in your physical body. Let your mind dwell on the amazing strength and vitality of the manifest Universe. You might want to picture horses galloping across a field, or children laughing and playing, or water thundering over Niagara Falls, or stars spinning through the vastness of space. Just dwell for a while on images that give you a feeling of strength and vitality. Then realize that this same strength, this same Almighty Life Force, is also working in and through you. Feel this Force—the ONE Force behind all of Creation—and know that it is surging through you right now. Feel how every cell and atom of your being thrills with health and strength. Allow yourself to enjoy this wonderful feeling of health and vitality. See yourself radiant and strong right now. Then give thanks because you now know that radiant health, strength and vitality are your True Nature.

No Doubts, Just Lots of Thanks

When you are finished, you can end your treatment by saying silently in your head or out loud: I give thanks that the Great Creative Power of the Universe—the ONE Life—is working in and through me right now, bringing me Life, Strength and Vitality. I give thanks for Perfect Health.

Then forget all about the matter until the next day. And do not doubt, but have perfect faith that your treatment is working.

In other words, just let the matter go and release your treatment to the Great Creative Power of the Universe with absolute certainty that the Universe will take care of the details.

Repeat Your Treatment

It's a good idea—especially if you are a beginner at all this—to repeat your treatment (the same treatment) every day for 30 days. And don't tell anyone what you are doing because this dissipates your power.

Just do it. In other words, know the Truth, be confident and have faith—and then forget all about your treatment. It's also important not to think about your problem or problems when you are not treating. If your problem enters your mind, switch your thoughts immediately to something else—to something positive and happy. (See the great Law of Substitution in Chapter 12 on The Power of Joy and Laughter.)

In other words, during the day, don't dwell on the problem you are treating for. Every time the thought pops up in your mind, switch your thoughts straight back to the Truth, i.e. the Nature of Reality. (See the power of The Seven Day Mental Diet in Chapter 4 on The Power of the Choice-Maker.) Get in touch with the big view of Life and of Your Life and the Universe. Then get on with your daily activities.

The Universe will take care of *how*. So don't bother to think about the details. (If you do, you dissipate the strength of your treatment by limiting the infinite number of ways in which the Universe can work things out.)

So treat and let go. If you do this consistently and wholeheartedly every day for 30 days, I guarantee you will be surprised at what happens.

Treating With Others

One of the most powerful forms of treatment is to treat with others. When you treat in a group, it's good to have a leader. Someone who can *speak the word* for the whole group. In other words, a group treatment is done aloud. (When you treat alone, by yourself, you do your treatment silently—going over things in your head.) In a group treatment, the leader speaks and everyone in the group repeats after the leader.

Small Groups

If you are treating in a small group (say 3–10 people), before you begin the treatment, you should ask everyone what they want to treat for. Obviously, you can only ask everyone if the group is small enough. Once everyone decides what they want to treat for, you are ready to begin.

But let's take a concrete example. In a group of four, John is the group leader.

John wants to treat for inspiration for an article he's writing, Mary wants to treat to heal her sore throat, Joe wants to treat to dissolve the tension between him and his boss at work, and Susan wants to treat for healing her relationship with her husband. After their specific treatments, everyone in the group wants to speak the word for Divine Intelligence to manifest in their lives.

Welcome the Great Creative Power
Once everyone has agreed upon what they want to treat for—all the people in the group sit comfortably in their chairs, relax, close their eyes and breathe deeply. Then John begins by saying...

This treatment is for Mary, Joe, Susan and John. (Everyone repeats after him)... The words that I speak are for Mary, Joe, Susan and John. I know that my words go out into the Great Universal Mind... and do not return to us void... but they accomplish the things of which I speak... (Everyone repeats)... I welcome the Great Universal Power... the Great Creative Power of the Universe... the ONE Life... And I give thanks... for all the blessings... in my life... I now focus my attention on... the ONE Life, which is perfect, whole and complete... I realize that this ONE perfect Life is animating and sustaining all of us... I realize that this ONE perfect Life is the unchanging principle of Perfect Good... and I know that this ONE perfect Life is now doing its perfect work in and through me...

John can go over everything that comes to his mind when he thinks about the ONE Life or the God Force that is behind everything in existence. In other words, he may continue until he gets a feeling that he has clarified his thoughts as to the Nature of Reality.

Speak the Word
When everyone in the group is relaxed and a feeling of harmony has settled over the room, John will then speak the word for each person. He will start by saying...

I now see the ONE Life working in and through Mary... (Everyone repeats, except Mary who says, "Working in and through me")... *I see this ONE Life animating Mary and every cell in Mary's body with its perfect vitality and intelligence... I see Mary full of health... and vitality... Mary's throat is strong... and healthy... every cell... in Mary's throat... is radiant and healthy... Mary's throat... is the healthiest of throats... a strong, robust, happy throat...* (When John feels enough has been said and everyone has a realization of the ONE Life working in and through Mary, he ends by saying)... *I have now spoken the word... for Mary's Life and health... and as this is a Divine Treatment... a Divine Activity... it cannot fail... And so it is...*

Then John goes on to the next person. In this case it's Joe's problem with his boss. In the same manner, John speaks the word for Joe by declaring and visualizing for Joe and the group how the ONE Life, which is peace and harmony, is establishing perfect peace between Joe and his boss. Then he speaks the word for harmony in Susan's relationship with her husband. Again he will describe the love and harmony of the ONE Life until the realization of love and harmony in Susan's relationship is firmly established in everyone's consciousness.

When it's time to speak the word for John, someone else in the group will lead the treatment for John who wants inspiration for the article he's writing.

Finally, when all the specific problems have been treated for, John then leads the group again and treats for Divine Intelligence which everyone in the group asked for at the beginning of this treatment. John ends the treatment by speaking the word for the whole world.

To conclude the treatment, John might say something like this...

I now speak the word... (Everyone repeats after him)... *for the whole world... I see the ONE Life Force working in and through*

every man, woman and child on Earth... I see all people...
everywhere... an expression of this ONE Life... living in Peace...
and Harmony... we see everyone... everywhere... full of Life...
healthy... happy... prosperous... loving... I see the Good coming
forth now. And as I see it, so it is.

Larger Groups

When treating in a larger group, it is not possible to *speak the*
word for everyone's specific request or problem. Instead here are
two ways to treat:

Method One: The whole group can treat for specific
demonstrations like Health, Divine Intelligence, Deep Peace,
Love, Prosperity—whatever the group agrees upon.

Method Two: Everyone in the group can write down what
they want to treat for on a piece of paper. Then everyone can
then hold their lists in their hands and the group can speak
the word for these lists to manifest.

Once again there should be a group leader who guides the group
through the treatment by speaking the word. As described above,
the leader should start by dwelling on the Nature of Reality to
help everyone clarify his or her thoughts about the ONE Life that
is animating and sustaining all of us. Then the leader can lead
the group and do a general treatment for specific qualities such
as Love, Intelligence, Radiant Health, Peace and Harmony—or
speak the word for manifestation of each person's list.

Again the leader should end the treatment by speaking
the word for the whole world and by giving thanks that this
treatment is a Divine activity and cannot fail.

Important Points When Treating

Keep your treatments simple.

Keep your treatments secret.

Relax. (Don't force things.)

Have perfect faith. (Do not doubt.)

Never instruct the Great Universal Power as to how you want things done.

Don't try to figure out how the things you've treated for will come to pass. (Leave the details to the Universe.)

Treat for results, not for the in between steps.

Forget all about your treatment when you're finished. (Release it and let it go.)

Don't dwell on your problems after you've treated them.

Go about your daily business as if the things you've treated for have already come to pass.

Then Give Thanks and Rejoice!

You will demonstrate, in other words, results will manifest in the outer world, when you know, realize or deeply "feel" the truth about the situation you are treating.

This means when you recognize and understand the Nature of Reality, when you see the Divine where you previously saw a problem or difficulty, your problem or difficulty will disappear!

So Rejoice... you just discovered the true meaning of Miracles!

15

The Power of the Good

Do you believe in a mixture of Good and evil?

Do you believe there's a constant struggle going on between Good and evil—and that it takes time for Good to manifest and win out over evil?

Do you believe it takes effort on your part to manifest Good in your life? Perhaps even extraordinary effort?

Come on now, let's face up to it. You probably do.

When embarking on the Road to Power, this is a typical beginner's mistake—based on a misunderstanding of the Nature of Reality. I remember thinking the same myself—that it takes a lot of effort to use these techniques and manifest new Good in my life. I remember thinking I had to try really hard.

This thought—that it takes effort to manifest Good in your life—stems from the belief in Good and evil. But if there is only Good, it takes no effort whatsoever on your part to manifest Good. Because if there is only Good, it means that the Good is pre-existent—that Good is all there is.

It just so happens that this is the case, which is Good news for all of us. Let me explain why this is true.

The Nature of Reality

The Nature of Reality is that behind the world of multiplicity that you seem to experience with your physical senses, there is a first cause—the ONE Force. The enlightened throughout the ages have called this ONE Force by various names such as God, the Creator, our Father, Brahman, the Force and numerous other names. Regardless of the name you choose to use, this ONE Force or Power is the cause back of all creation.

To simplify our exploration, let us call this first cause the "ONE."

Now it is crucial to your understanding and effective use of all the techniques described in this book, to understand the nature of this ONE. So let us analyze what ONE really means.

To begin with, since this ONE Force or Power created all there is, we can deduce that this ONE must also be all there is. In other words, this ONE must be all of It—all of existence—all of Life itself. Nothing exists but this ONE, which is all there is.

We cannot go further back than this.

This must mean that since this ONE is the only Life there is, It must be everywhere present—and in everything. So we can say that this ONE is the animating Force behind all of creation. In other words, this ONE is the First Cause. This ONE—which many call God or the Force—is the Cause, the Origin and the Originator of all creation.

The ONE

Now since this ONE is the First Cause and Origin of all there is, it means there is no opposing force—and that there can never be an opposing force because there is only the ONE. This is an extremely important point to understand because all further realization is based on understanding this concept. So I repeat: There is nothing in existence but this ONE. And since there is only ONE First Cause and Originator, only ONE Life and ONE animating force, it means there is no opposing force. If there were an opposing force, it would mean there had to be "two"—two forces.

The idea or belief in "two" is the basis of any and all belief in Good and evil. Please ponder on this.

The Field

This idea of ONE is also confirmed by quantum physics and the theory of the unified field. According to the latest scientific research, all of manifest creation is one vast field of energy. Physicists say that the atoms that make up you, me and everything else in our world are all identical and interchangeable. Moreover, these identical and interchangeable atoms are made up of the same identical and interchangeable subatomic particles, which all can be broken down into waves of energy. These waves of energy are what form the one interconnected unified field, which gives rise to all of creation.

Many of our great spiritual, metaphysical and esoteric teachers have long taught that behind all of manifest creation, there is the one etheric field in which we all live and move and have our being. Scientists may be on the verge of identifying this field.

The Nature of the ONE Field

Let us continue our exploration of the Nature of the ONE and examine some of the characteristics of the ONE that is All of It.

If there is only ONE, then ONE must be:

Omnipotent / all-powerful: This is because if there is only ONE and this ONE is All there Is, there is no opposing force as we just mentioned. This means that since there is nothing to oppose or resist this ONE, this ONE Life must be all-powerful. In other words, the ONE is not some power, but All the Power There Is. In other words, the ONE is omnipotent.

Omnipresent / all-present: Since the ONE Life is all there is, It must be fully present everywhere throughout all of creation. In other words, it must be all-present—omnipresent. Thus the same ONE Life is animating all of creation, including you, me—and everyone and everything.

Omniscient / all-knowing: Since the ONE is all there is, it must also be Infinite Mind or Intelligence since It conceived of, created and contains all of creation. In other words, the ONE is omniscient. It knows everything there is to know since it created All of It.

Peace and harmony: When there is only ONE, there is no conflict because there is no opposing force. Thus the ONE must be the one action or activity which is peace and harmony.

Love: Love is another word for peace, harmony. Love is the word we use to describe perfect safety, comfort, protection, when all is balance and harmony. What can be more safe than being All of It?

Abundance: Since all of creation is contained within the ONE, the ONE must be infinite abundance. Because it is All of It.

Indestructible: Since there is nothing to oppose the ONE, it must be indestructible. There is no other force, which can harm or destroy this field.

Immortal / Eternal: Since the ONE is indestructible, it must also be immortal or eternal. In other words, the ONE must be the ONE eternal Life, which never dies. Or we could say the ONE is birthless and deathless.

Principle: A principle or law is something, which never changes. Thus we can see that since this ONE is eternal and immortal, it must be principle or law because it is unchanging. (See my book *The Awakening Human Being – A Guide to the Power of Mind* for a detailed explanation of the concept of principle.)

Perfect Good: From all this we can deduce that since this ONE is all that exists, It must be the unchanging Principle of Perfect Good.

Why Good?

Let us define Good. What is Good? What is your definition of *Good*? Your definition of the Highest Good you can conceive of?

Your definition of the Highest Good is the same as everyone else's definition. The Highest Good you can conceive of is unlimited Life, unlimited Love, unlimited Peace and Harmony, unlimited Abundance. And as we have just seen, all of these definitions of the Highest Good are the characteristics of the ONE—the ONE in which we all live and move and have our being.

This is our line of reasoning. This is how we know that the ONE is the unchanging Principle of Perfect Good.

All Is Good

This means that since the ONE which is All of It is Good, that All is Good.

What a relief!

Now you know that you don't have to create the Good!

The Good is already there!

So it's not up to you. You don't have to try to create Good.

The Good was there to begin with. The Good is here now. The Good is All there Is.

So the burden is not on your shoulders.

Good is the Nature of Reality. The Nature of Reality is Good—because the ONE that creates, animates and sustains All of us and All of It—is Good. There is in fact nothing else.

This makes changing your Life—bringing new Good into your Life—easy. All you have to do is focus your attention on the Good—on the Nature of Reality—and let it appear.

Most of us have a tendency to think that creating the Good is our responsibility. Something we must use a lot of effort to achieve. But that is not the case as you now understand. The Good is already here now. You don't have to create it, but you must stop limiting the manifestation of Good in your life by focusing your attention on limitation. This is your only task!

That's why changing your life—bringing new Good into your life—is so easy. You could say all you have to do is surrender to the Good!

What Is Real?

Here is another way of coming to the same conclusion about the Nature of Reality.

This time, let us use another line of reasoning and start at the beginning again with the question: What is real?

If we define "real" as that which never changes, we can start by asking ourselves—what never changes? If you follow this line of reasoning, you will quickly discover that everything in the physical world changes. The weather changes, people change, situations change—everything in the physical world is in a state of constant flux. When we think about ourselves, we discover that we too are in a state of constant flux. Our bodies are changing, our emotions are changing, our thoughts are changing, our ideas and opinions are changing, our actions are changing—in other words, everything we experience is changing too.

If you keep on questioning yourself, you will discover there is only one thing, which does not change—and that is your awareness of *being here*. You are aware—you are awareness itself—whether you are thinking happy thoughts or sad thoughts. You are awareness itself whether you are having a good day or a bad day. You are awareness itself whether you are rich or poor, young or old, man or woman. If you focus your attention on this awareness, you will discover that you are aware of the fact that you are here now, no matter what you are feeling. It makes no difference to this sense of awareness if you are feeling vibrantly healthy or miserably ill. You are still aware. This awareness—this consciousness, this witnessing—this sense of being *you*—of beingness—does not disappear or change, regardless of your changing thoughts, emotions or actions. This beingness of you is always there. It is the one thing that remains constant at all times. So from this we can deduce that *this sense of beingness is real*. In other words, this sense of beingness that we all experience, is the only thing we can know for sure. The only thing we can know with 100% certainty.

If you do not see this, take a moment now to ask yourself what you know for sure. What do you know of—with complete certainty—that never changes? If you do this, you will discover that the only thing you know with 100% certainty is the fact that *you are*. We could say that *you are* is proof of your own existence! Nothing else proves that you are real!

Your I AM Presence

Another word or expression we can use for this sense of beingness that we all experience is the phrase—the "I AM" presence. Our I AM presence is a way of expressing this beingness—this unlimited beingness—in words. This is because to say I AM alone, expresses this sense of beingness without limitation or you could say without definition. As soon as you add a suffix to I AM—as soon as you say I AM happy or I AM sad—you are qualifying this sense of beingness (and limiting it) with a definition of a state which will sooner or later change into something else. But the phrase I AM expresses unlimited beingness.

What Is This I AM Presence?

So what is this I AM presence? As we just determined, this I AM presence is your sense of unqualified beingness. Your sense of pure consciousness—pure, unqualified awareness. Further back in our exploration of the Nature of Reality we cannot go. You cannot go beyond this sense of beingness. Thus the great thinkers of the world have deduced that this consciousness, this awareness you are experiencing here and now, must be identical with the ONE we discussed at the beginning of this chapter. If this was not true, how could we exist? This consciousness is what we are. And since we are part of the ONE, the ONE must be this consciousness.

We Are Good!

Thus if we continue with our line of reasoning, we arrive at the logical conclusion that since we are identical with consciousness, which is the ONE and the ONE is All there Is, then we must have the same characteristics as the ONE. Thus, we can conclude that we, like the ONE, must be GOOD!

But what does all this mean for you in practical terms? How is this understanding going to improve your Life?

In brief this understanding can radically change your life because since you are the Choice-Maker in your life (see Chapter 4 on The Power of the Choice-Maker) you have free will to direct the focus of your attention. This means you can now choose to either continue to think limiting thoughts about yourself and about Life and experience their manifestation in your life— or you can choose to align your thoughts with the Nature of Reality. When you choose to align your thoughts with the Nature of Reality, you are aligning yourself with the *all-powerful ONE*, which we now know is unlimited intelligence, unlimited Life, unlimited Love, unlimited peace, unlimited harmony, unlimited abundance, in short—unlimited Good.

This focus will alter everything in your Life.

16

The Power of Our Teachers

We are blessed to have so many wonderful teachers. Here are some of my favorite teachers and their books:

Frederick Bailes
Your Mind Can Heal You
Basic Principles of the Science of Mind

Deepak Chopra
The Seven Spiritual Laws of Success
Creating Affluence
Ageless Body, Timeless Mind
+ all his other books and tapes

A Course in Miracles

Mary Baker Eddy
Science and Health
+ all her other books

Emmanuel's books
Emmanuel's Book – A Manual for Living Comfortably in the Cosmos
Emmanuel's Book II – The Choice for Love
Emmanuel's Book III – What Is an Angel Doing Here?

Findhorn books
The Findhorn Garden: Pioneering a New Vision of Man and Nature in Cooperation and the **Eileen Caddy** books.

Emmet Fox
Power Through Constructive Thinking
Make Your Life Worthwhile
Alter Your Life
Find and Use Your Inner Power
+ all his other books

Thich Nhat Hanh
Being Peace
Peace Is Every Step
+ all his other books

David R. Hawkins
Power vs. Force
Success Is for You
+ all his other books

Louise L. Hay
You Can Heal Your Life
Life! Reflections on Your Journey
The Power Is Within You
Heal Your Body
+ all her other books and tapes

Esther and Jerry Hicks (The Teachings of Abraham)
Ask and It Is Given
The Law of Attraction
+ all their other books

Napoleon Hill
Think and Grow Rich
The Master Key to Riches
+ all his other books

Ernest Holmes
The Science of Mind
Living the Science of Mind
Creative Mind and Success
Ideas of Power
The Anatomy of Healing Prayer
+ all his other books

Emma Curtis Hopkins
Scientific Christian Mental Practice
High Mysticism

Barbara Marx Hubbard
Happy Birthday Planet Earth
The Hunger of Eve

Byron Katie
Loving What Is
I Need Your Love
A Thousand Names for Joy

Dalai Lama
The Art of Happiness
Ethics for the New Millennium
+ all his other books

Shirley MacLaine
Out on a Limb (the book and the movie)
+ all her other books

Sri Nisargadatta Maharaj
I Am That
+ all his other books

David Malin
A View of the Universe

Catherine Ponder
The Dynamic Laws of Prosperity
The Prosperity Secrets of the Ages
The Dynamic Laws of Healing
The Healing Secrets of the Ages
+ all her other books

Tim Ray
Starbrow: A Spiritual Adventure
Starwarrior: A Spiritual Thriller

James Redfield
The Celestine Prophecy: An Adventure
The Celestine Prophecy: An Experiential Guide
(with Carol Adrienne)

Florence Scovel Shinn
The Game of Life and How to Play It
The Power of the Spoken Word
The Secret Door to Success
Your Word Is Your Wand

Jose Silva
The Silva Mind Control Method
You the Healer (with Robert B. Stone)
+ all his other books

Jon P. Speller
Seed Money in Action: Working the Law of Tenfold Return

J.R.R. Tolkien
The Lord of the Rings
The Hobbit
+ all his other books, poetry, songs

Eckhart Tolle
The Power of Now
A New Earth
+ all his other books

Neale Donald Walsch
Conversations with God (Vol. 1–3)
+ all his other books

Stuart Wilde
The Force
Miracles
The Trick to Money Is Having Some!
+ all his other books and tapes

Marianne Williamson
A Return to Love
Illuminata: Thoughts, Prayers, Rites of Passage
+ all her other books and tapes

17

The Power of the Vision

What is the next step?
Where are we all going?

We are witnessing... and participating in... great events, extraordinary events. Nothing less than a planetary transformation is taking place, right here and now. Nothing less than a revolution in consciousness is going on.

This is A Time of Great Awakening!
Hallelujah!

Humanity has moved—more or less—from an intuitive, group-oriented, tribal consciousness, which lived in harmony with nature (as all natural tribal people did, e.g. the Native Americans, the Aborigines, the Eskimos, etc.) for countless generations to an individualized, ego-based consciousness, which spread out aggressively from Europe and conquered the tribal peoples of the world by unleashing the enormous powers of science and technology. This ego-based consciousness, with its focus on the individual and the material world, mastered the planet by developing our intellectual and analytical abilities.

Now this ego-based, analytical orientation—this secular worldview called scientific materialism—having served its purpose by unleashing the vast powers of science and technology has gone amok. Greed, selfishness, war, pollution, violence, profit without thought for the well-being of the Planet... you know the story. We all know the story. And we all know that we cannot continue in this direction any longer without self-destructing pretty soon.

Add to the world situation we have created, the fact that scientific discoveries now clearly demonstrate that the "materialism" upon which this secular worldview is based was incorrect. It turns out that the Mystics were right: We *are* all bodies of Light. We *are* all interconnected patterns of energy. The universe *is* a massive energy system in which the observer participates. In short, there is no so-called "objective" world out there, which can be measured independently of the observer. Instead science now tells us that our reality *is* in fact the result of our intentions. (Hallelujah again!)

So obviously it's time for a change in our orientation. Time for a planetary shift, a massive transformation in our collective consciousness. Which might explain why there are so many souls gathered on the Planet right now. It's as if we all decided to come here to join the party!

Undoubtedly, the analytical mind has done its work: We've opened new doors, we've liberated enormous powers. But now we need to re-orient and use more than our analytical minds— we need to listen to our hearts once again. We need to tune into that inner voice and get in touch with our True Selves so that we have the necessary *vision* to take control of our creations.

Yes, it's time. It's time.

It's time we grow up and take the next step in our evolution and become the *Conscious Choice-makers*, not only in our own lives, but in the planetary life of our species. Because yes, we are the Guardians of the Sacred Fire now. We are grown up now. We are all Co-Creators with the Force.

But to take the next step, to take our rightful place in the Universe as Co-Creators, we must have the *vision*.

Many are using the techniques described in my books and in other books to re-orient their own consciousness and their own lives. And this of course is fine because individual re-orientation is basic to the survival of the Planet. So of course, this is the first, crucial step.

You must get your own house in order first.

You must become the Conscious Choice-Maker in your own life, first. Because until you do this, until you attune yourself to a higher energy level, you can do nothing. All your dreams and good wishes and good intentions for Planet Earth will amount to nothing if your own house is in shambles. ("By their fruits ye shall know them." Matthew 7:20)

But when your own house is in order, when you can no longer contain the joy of living which fills your soul. When this joy bursts forth in your Life, then you'll find that you're definitely ready for the next step. Because joy is expansive and cannot be contained! Oh yes, you know how it feels... Joy is compelling, irresistible and catching! Joy is joy, something you automatically want to share with everyone you meet. Something you want to infect your neighbors with. Something you can't contain or resist... something wonderful...

Real Love, Divine Love, Universal Love,
according to Frederick Bailes,
is
"the intense desire for the well-being of others!"

What a marvelous definition!

What Next?

So what are we supposed to do now? How are we supposed to live, on a daily basis, as Co-Creators with the Force, as the Conscious Choice-Makers in our own Lives and in the Life of the Planet?

First of all, we must remember the Nature of the Universe: *The Thought always comes first. Thought is the first cause.* Thought is the First Cause, in your Life and in the Life of the Planet and in the Life of the Universe. And since Thought is the *first cause,* we must, first of all, have the Thought. The Right Thought. The

Clear, Focused Thought. This means it's so important that we train ourselves to think clearly and envision Good. We must see in our mind's eye a clear vision of the New World before it can manifest and become reality.

In other words, we must conceive it and believe it first. Then and only then will it appear on the outer plane. Then and only then, when the vision is clear and strong—and we know it and believe it—will it manifest. So it's vitally important that we do the inner work for Planetary Transformation right now and maintain a clear vision in our daily lives of where we're going.

How Are We Supposed to Live?

How then do enlightened men and women actually live?

Ask yourself.

Meditate on this question.

Find concrete answers.

Find solutions that you know in your heart will work.

This is what I envision:

First of all, life on Planet Earth, humanity as we know it, is evolving. This means we *are* capable of evolving, becoming better, higher, more loving.

This also means that enlightened men and women are practicing and will continue to practice the Golden Rule of Jesus on a daily basis, every minute, every hour of every day. We must "do unto others"... There is no other way, no other viable solution for ourselves or for the Planet.

And this "doing unto others" includes right thinking, too, since Thought is the Seed of Reality. In the next stage of our evolution our thoughts will be visible. (For those who are sensitive, they already are.) Thus... doing unto others includes envisioning and seeking for others the very same Good that we envision and seek for ourselves. Yes, the Good of One is the Good of All.

This also means seeing the Divine in everyone, including

people we dislike and our so-called "enemies." We may condemn the way other people behave. In other words, we may dislike the outer man or woman and denounce his or her behavior, but we must recognize and salute, at all times, the Divinity within each and every person we meet on our way. We must wish them well and envision the Highest Good for them too, or again as Frederick Bailes put it, constantly entertain "an intense desire for the well-being of others."

With this in mind, we will always make the right choices, for ourselves and the Planet.

Recycle Your Garbage

When we know and see ourselves as the Conscious Choice-Makers in our lives and in the Life of the Planet, of course we'll think about the consequences of our actions. All our actions. In practical terms, this means we'll recycle our garbage, save water, eat organic foods, buy environment-friendly houses, conserve our forests, put environment-friendly toner in our printers, ride bikes, clean up the oceans, drive environment-friendly cars, support sustainable growth projects, wear clothes made of organic cotton or recycled cans, buy natural cosmetics, stop smoking, support quality and craftsmanship, boycott products which are hazardous to our health and the health of the Planet, practice deep peace, eat less, plant and hug trees, heal our bodies, practice silence, circulate our money and resources and energy, tithe, listen to the wisdom of our hearts, and use our unique talents to do righteous work for righteous companies and decent, honest, ethical humane organizations. In other words, we will give and love and give and love and give and love some more...

It goes without saying doesn't it? That the Conscious Choice-Maker is conscious of what he or she does and how it affects the Whole, the Unity of All of Us, each and every step of the way, each and every moment of every day.

Listen to Barbara Marx Hubbard

No one says it better than Futurist Barbara Marx Hubbard in her book *Happy Birthday Planet Earth*. This is her call to all of us:

Think carefully. Think clearly. Think aspirationally. Focus upon your vision of what you want to become. Ask your inner calling to speak to you. Let the compass of joy guide your thoughts till they focus on the magnetic attraction for a creative act in the world.

What are you born to do? Imagine yourself doing your heart's desire. Conceive yourself doing everything you ever dreamed of doing, being everything you ever dreamed of being.

Place that vision in the context of the evolution of humankind toward *full* humanity. See yourself participating in that evolution, joining with all others also responding to a unique call from within.

Make That Shift Right Now

Now is the time to practice Right Thinking. Now is the time to focus the power of your thoughts on the Highest and Best you can conceive of. Now is the time to move from old, outdated, worn-out models of existence and ego-based competition to actions which are in harmony with Nature and which promote love, health, peace and harmony among all Creatures and Beings on the Planet—for the Highest Good of All Concerned.

And make sure your thoughts are always Positive, Constructive, Beneficial and Specific in all of their aspects. For yourself and for everyone else. Use your power as a Conscious Choice-Maker wisely. Envision and manifest Deep Peace, Wisdom and Understanding, Perfect Health, Inexhaustible Vitality, Unshakable Joy, Wealth, Prosperity and Overflowing Abundance for yourself and for everyone else on the Planet.

Feel the Joy

Think positively about the Planetary Shift in Consciousness that is taking place right now. See it happening. Feel it happening. Feel the *Joy* of it. Know in your Heart of Hearts that we, together, we the Conscious Choice-Makers, are now transforming Planet Earth, our home, into the Heavenly Paradise we see in our Minds' Eyes. See it, feel it and believe it… and it will manifest.

Because, yes, we are the *First Cause*.

And because yes, yes indeed, we are, all together now, Divine Spirits, who are singing and dancing, on the Road to Power!

And so it is.

Hallelujah!

BOOKS

O-BOOKS

SPIRITUALITY

O is a symbol of the world, of oneness and unity; this eye represents knowledge and insight. We publish titles on general spirituality and living a spiritual life. We aim to inform and help you on your own journey in this life.
If you have enjoyed this book, why not tell other readers by posting a review on your preferred book site? Recent bestsellers from O-Books are:

Heart of Tantric Sex
Diana Richardson
Revealing Eastern secrets of deep love and intimacy to Western couples.
Paperback: 978-1-90381-637-0 ebook: 978-1-84694-637-0

Crystal Prescriptions
The A-Z guide to over 1,200 symptoms
and their healing crystals
Judy Hall
The first in the popular series of six books,
this handy little guide is packed as tight as a pill-bottle with crystal remedies for ailments.
Paperback: 978-1-90504-740-6 ebook: 978-1-84694-629-5

Take Me To Truth
Undoing the Ego
Nouk Sanchez, Tomas Vieira
The best-selling step-by-step book on shedding the Ego,
using the teachings of *A Course In Miracles*.
Paperback: 978-1-84694-050-7 ebook: 978-1-84694-654-7

The 7 Myths about Love...Actually!
The journey from your HEAD to the HEART of your SOUL
Mike George
Smashes all the myths about LOVE.
Paperback: 978-1-84694-288-4 ebook: 978-1-84694-682-0

The Holy Spirit's Interpretation of the New Testament
A course in Understanding and Acceptance
Regina Dawn Akers
Following on from the strength of *A Course In Miracles*, NTI
teaches us how to experience the love and oneness of God.
Paperback: 978-1-84694-085-9 ebook: 978-1-78099-083-5

The Message of A Course In Miracles
A translation of the text in plain language
Elizabeth A. Cronkhite
A translation of *A Course in Miracles* into plain, everyday
language for anyone seeking inner peace. The companion
volume, *Practicing A Course In Miracles*, offers practical
lessons and mentoring.
Paperback: 978-1-84694-319-5 ebook: 978-1-84694-642-4

Rising in Love
My Wild and Crazy Ride to Here and Now, with Amma,
the Hugging Saint
Ram Das Batchelder
Rising in Love conveys an author's extraordinary journey

of spiritual awakening with the Guru, Amma.
Paperback: 978-1-78279-687-9 ebook: 978-1-78279-686-2

Thinker's Guide to God
Peter Vardy
An introduction to key issues in the philosophy of religion.
Paperback: 978-1-90381-622-6

Your Simple Path
Find happiness in every step
Ian Tucker
A guide to helping us reconnect with what is really
important in our lives.
Paperback: 978-1-78279-349-6 ebook: 978-1-78279-348-9

365 Days of Wisdom
Daily Messages To Inspire You Through The Year
Dadi Janki
Daily messages which cool the mind, warm the heart
and guide you along your journey.
Paperback: 978-1-84694-863-3 ebook: 978-1-84694-864-0

Body of Wisdom
Women's Spiritual Power and How it Serves
Hilary Hart
Bringing together the dreams and experiences of women across
the world with today's most visionary spiritual teachers.
Paperback: 978-1-78099-696-7 ebook: 978-1-78099-695-0

Dying to Be Free
From Enforced Secrecy to Near Death to True Transformation
Hannah Robinson
After an unexpected accident and near-death experience,
Hannah Robinson found herself radically transforming her life,

while a remarkable new insight altered her relationship
with her father, a practising Catholic priest.
Paperback: 978-1-78535-254-6 ebook: 978-1-78535-255-3

The Ecology of the Soul
A Manual of Peace, Power and Personal Growth
for Real People in the Real World
Aidan Walker
Balance your own inner Ecology of the Soul to regain
your natural state of peace, power and wellbeing.
Paperback: 978-1-78279-850-7 ebook: 978-1-78279-849-1

Not I, Not other than I
The Life and Teachings of Russel Williams
Steve Taylor, Russel Williams
The miraculous life and inspiring teachings
of one of the World's greatest living Sages.
Paperback: 978-1-78279-729-6 ebook: 978-1-78279-728-9

On the Other Side of Love
A Woman's Unconventional Journey Towards Wisdom
Muriel Maufroy
When life has lost all meaning, what do you do?
Paperback: 978-1-78535-281-2 ebook: 978-1-78535-282-9

Practicing A Course In Miracles
A Translation of the Workbook in Plain Language
and With Mentoring Notes
Elizabeth A. Cronkhite
The practical second and third volumes of The Plain-Language
A Course In Miracles.
Paperback: 978-1-84694-403-1 ebook: 978-1-78099-072-9

Quantum Bliss
The Quantum Mechanics of Happiness, Abundance, and Health
George S. Mentz
Quantum Bliss is the breakthrough summary of success and
spirituality secrets that customers have been waiting for.
Paperback: 978-1-78535-203-4 ebook: 978-1-78535-204-1

The Upside Down Mountain
Mags MacKean
A must-read for anyone weary of chasing success and
happiness – one woman's inspirational journey swapping
the uphill slog for the downhill slope.
Paperback: 978-1-78535-171-6 ebook: 978-1-78535-172-3

Your Personal Tuning Fork
The Endocrine System
Deborah Bates
Discover your body's health secret, the endocrine system,
and 'twang' your way to sustainable health!
Paperback: 978-1-84694-503-8 ebook: 978-1-78099-697-4

Readers of ebooks can buy or view any of these bestsellers by
clicking on the live link in the title. Most titles are published
in paperback and as an ebook. Paperbacks are available in
traditional bookshops. Both print and ebook formats are
available online.

Find more titles and sign up to our readers' newsletter at
http://www.johnhuntpublishing.com/mind-body-spirit

Follow us on Facebook at
https://www.facebook.com/OBooks/
and Twitter at https://twitter.com/obooks